D0679481

S

S-11

Art Education

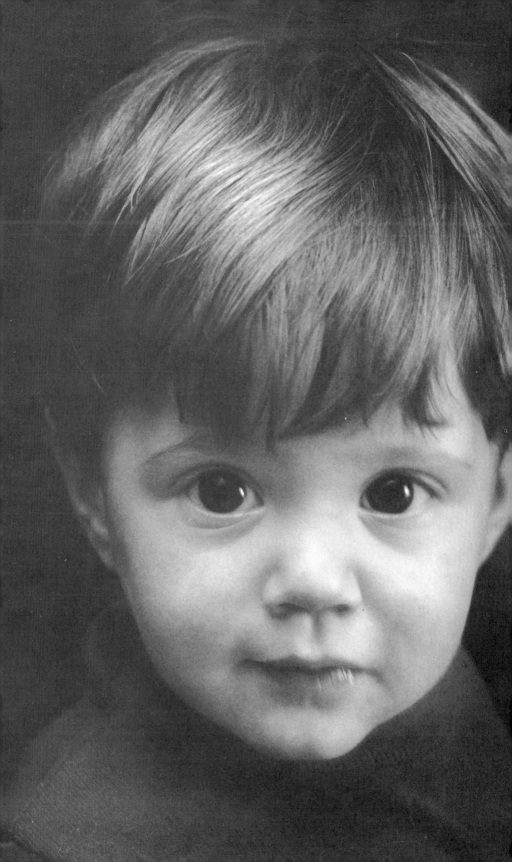

Art Education: Strategies of Teaching

MARK LUCA
University of California

ROBERT KENT
University of Georgia

PRENTICE-HALL, INC., ENGLEWOOD CLIFFS, NEW JERSEY

MODERN ELEMENTARY METHODS SERIES

© 1968 by Prentice-Hall, Inc.
Englewood Cliffs, New Jersey

*All rights reserved. No part of this
book may be reproduced in any form or by
any means without permission in
writing from the publisher.*

Photographs by
RODOLFO PETSCHEK & ELOISE WILLIAMS RIVERA

Current printing (last digit):
10   9   8   7   6   5   4   3   2

*Library of Congress
Catalog Card Number: 68–20766*

PRENTICE-HALL INTERNATIONAL, INC., *London*
PRENTICE-HALL OF AUSTRALIA, PTY. LTD., *Sydney*
PRENTICE-HALL OF CANADA, LTD., *Toronto*
PRENTICE-HALL OF INDIA PRIVATE LTD., *New Delhi*
PRENTICE-HALL OF JAPAN, INC., *Tokyo*

Printed in the United States of America

ANDERSON COLLEGE
LIBRARY
ANDERSON, INDIANA

N
36½
.L8
1968

Preface

The world of art and the world of art education are, unfortunately, in separated camps. Yet each needs the other. In this book the authors attempt to see the arts, the schools, and society in a unified backdrop and they hope to show how the separate camps can work together under unified aims.

Even though it takes children several years to learn to read, write and to use arithmetic effectively, the language of art is natural to children before they enter school. No matter how high or (within limits) how low the I.Q. or how mature or immature a child is when he enters school he usually can draw with joy and ease. However, with improper or no art education, children "lose" their ability to draw and construct and their art progress is halted as they grow older. With such children, their inabilities in art intensify until most adults have become "illiterates" in the visual language. In this book we hope to demonstrate, (1) how our art heritage can become part of the art education curriculum; (2) how a developmental and individualized art program relates to the needs and expectations of the growing child; (3) how the teacher and the staff can, in a classroom setting, effect a good art program; (4) how we can look beyond the immediate and practical curriculum to a changing and more progressive art education in the future.

Following are some acknowledgments we would like to make. To Professor John Michaelis of the University of California at Berkeley, who first suggested that we write the book

v

ANDERSON COLLEGE
LIBRARY
ANDERSON, INDIANA

79249

and who has given us valuable advice throughout the process. Susan Luca and Celeste Kent, who helped with typing and editing, have our gratitude.

We were fortunate to secure two photographers who understand art and children and who take the art of photography seriously.

Photographs by Rodolfo Petschek: frontispiece, pages 3, 27, 35, 39, 53, 61, 70, 76, and 86.

Photographs by Eloise Rivera: pages 9, 16, 21, and 48.

Frontispiece — Hans, age 4.
p. 3   — Tempera painting by Maria, age 6.
p. 9   — Crayon drawing by Molly, age 5.
p. 16   — Papier maché by Greg, age 7.
p. 21   — Water color by Andy, age 8.
p. 27   — Ceramic head by Liz, age 11.
p. 35   — Wood sculpture by Darryl, age 11.
p. 39   — Painted stone by Raul, age 10.
p. 48   — Clay by Molly, age 5.
p. 53   — Clay pot by Mark, age 10.
p. 61   — Clay on a wheel, Kurt, age 12.
p. 70   — Wire and cloth maché from San Francisco children's art class.
p. 76   — Clay, Karen, age 9.
p. 86   — Mike, age 10.

MARK LUCA
ROBERT KENT

Contents

Art Education

CHAPTER ONE

Introduction and Foundations

Today a bewildering array of new concepts and innovations is rapidly emerging in American education. How these changes will affect the elementary art program is the major concern of this book.

Some of the innovations now in operation or in the planning stages fall into the following categories: (1) organization of the structure of knowledge for curriculum planning; (2) formation of independent educational research and development teams at state and local levels; (3) imaginative uses of new equipment and educational resources; and (4) radical changes in the structure of the school program, such as the nongraded school, flexible scheduling, and master teacher or teacher resource programs. These innovations have an influence on art education.

Never has the interest and research activity in creativity been as high. Not only is this true in art education but in almost every field of endeavor in and out of school. Grave concerns have been expressed about the lack of cultural resources in cities, satellite communities, and in remote rural areas.

The art educator's task is first to introduce art as a visual language and then to help develop and exercise the students' perceptual capacities. Next he must introduce students to man's cultural heritage, develop their personal aesthetic and critical awareness, and help them to achieve personal and cultural identity by developing skills in art commensurate with their abilities.

1

Our society is characterized by a burgeoning science technology that unfortunately demands quantitative instead of qualitative evaluation for economic and social success. At the same time we are witnessing a booming but erratic cultural explosion that needs aesthetic guidelines and priorities.

Schools are constantly being challenged by various groups that would have art thrown out of the school program as an unnecessary frill, or by others who want to retain an art program but would shape it into empty conformity. The public should be educated and alerted to the dangers of an emasculated art program, and the steady erosion of aesthetic values already too painfully evident in the despoilation of our rapidly vanishing natural resources and in the flood of tasteless products being spewed forth to an aesthetically dormant consumer.

How can this be accomplished? First, art educators in cooperation with school administrators must be prepared to assume leadership in explaining and defending to legislators, boards of education, and the public the importance of the visual arts and visual education to all children in order for them more fully to explore the varieties, complexities, and vast dimensions of today's society. Second, art educators must point out to all who will listen that art is a basic means of man's communication that relies on both cognition and emotion to make its greatest impact on the sensitivities of man. And third, they must affirm that art can help enliven and enlighten the child's quest for beauty and order in a world already too heavily burdened and apprehensive over the imbalance of scientific dominance.

The authors believe that there is an art to teaching art. The elementary art teacher must have more than a modest desire to teach art and must be technically competent, having received professional training in studio art classes. He should have at his command a broad understanding of art history and should be required to study art education as a major field, involving historical, philosophical, psychological, and sociological inquiry. And last, the art teacher must have a strong commitment to the world of art, not only vicariously but as an active participant in a creative enterprise.

New Trends, Practices, and Objectives

CHAPTER TWO

THE STRUCTURE OF ART

Art, the Subject

Art has existed in a continuum throughout history, either in the context of tribal ritual or in individual determinism, and it is the latter aspect that has become so dominant today. It has only been recently that child art has been recognized as an important activity and as having an intimate relationship to art as seen by the anthropologist and the professional artist. The work of both the artist and the child are byproducts of cognitive and affective processes. It is evident that art is both an intellectual and an emotional expression of an attitude or experience that is usually presented in a personal manner.

There is a distinct difference between the nature of art and the natures of music (which depends primarily on auditory stimuli and a persistent time dimension) and literature (which depends on the stringing together of arbitrary symbols within a time sequence that is more predetermined than art). Whether two- or three-dimensional, art appeals primarily to the eyes, and its manner and sequence are less predictable than those of the other creative forms. It is less dependent upon a formal time structure. Whether simple or sophisticated, whether by a capable professional or a spontaneous child—the very nature of the art medium has certain unique characteristics. An art work is either in black and white or totally or partly in color (having *hue*, the name of the color; *value*, the lightness or darkness of the color; and *intensity*, the color brightness). *Line* can play a very dominant role in abstract or nonobjective works or it can be subdued or eliminated. *Form* is the name

4

given to the shape, or the area of delineations. *Texture*, though it may be perceived only through the eyes, can give the illusion of touch.

Whatever art material is used (crayon, oil, fresco, clay, etc.), the interrelationship or arrangement makes for the *composition*. This is determined by what the composer wants to communicate. In analyzing the success of a given composition, the evaluator, whether a well-seasoned critic or a teacher, is governed by personal prejudices and the forces of the cultural style preferences that surround him. A highly popular and highly praised work of one generation or country would be a forgotten failure in another circumstance. It is common to use descriptive words like *dominance, subordination, proportion, rhythm, balance, repetition*, etc., but here too, it is impossible to have agreement upon qualitative standards of excellence. The best guide is the sum of the general agreement of the opinions of leaders in the field. The ultimate guide of a work in progress by a child or an artist, however, should be his intuitive and personal feeling of rightness. But the child, being more limited than the artist, needs more guidance. After the work is "cold" it can be left to the test of time.

The work of art represents one of man's highest achievements. Past civilizations, with their trappings of politics and military conquests, have been swept into the ashcans of history. However, many of these civilizations have left us artistic records of their people's dreams and thoughts, and because of this man has had the opportunity continually to experience the greatness of older cultures and to benefit from their artistic endeavors in light of his present-day perceptions.

Today, the American schools not only have the capability but have the greatest responsibility to assume a more vigorous role in preparing school children for visual learning through processes of education.

Even though there have been setbacks, art education has advanced on many fronts. For example, recent research by McFee, Burkhart, Barron, MacKinnon, and Guilford has done much to explain the nature of the creative process. We have learned that the creative potential of most children must be stimulated and constantly exercised in order to function. The development of the creative potential of all children must be one of the prime objectives of art education in the elementary schools.

Though there has been substantial progress in art education at the theoretical levels, there is still a very noticeable lag between research and everyday classroom practices. This is quite evident in two specific areas: the complexities of aesthetic preferences and the understanding of perceptual discriminations.

Of great interest to art educators is the work of Jean Piaget, the Swiss psychologist, educator, and philosopher. In the past forty years he has produced some of the most systematic and comprehensive theories of cognitive development. His theories explain the evolution of language and thought in children. Most pertinent to art educators is his investigation into the child's conception of space. His studies have reinforced the already known concept that children perceive things differently than do adults. Piaget's work suggests the possibility of establishing a program of art readiness similar to reading readiness, in which the child would be helped to develop his ideas of spacial concepts as the result of visual and motor action. His studies suggest that art educators have been too prone to promote the child's emotional output as the only valid means of artistic expression. However, it should be pointed out that although the cognitive aspects of teaching art are important in building a storehouse of visual perceptions, art educators should not de-emphasize the emotional and metaphorical characteristics inherent in much of children's art.

In recent years art educators have made great use of new developments in instructional media. The imaginative use of closed circuit television, multiple slide projectors, and a more creative use of standard audio-visual equipment have greatly expanded the means of teaching art to more children. Parallel to this has been the art educator's desire to utilize the resources of the community—to bring professional artists into the classroom, and to rely on scholars outside the field of art education for help in curriculum development, the psychology of learning, and the process of decision-making in both teaching and administering the art program.

Throughout history, basic concepts of art have always been expressed through the recognition of formal values as the underlying structure of the aesthetic experience. It can be said that the objects per se, that is, paintings, sculpture, architecture, do not express by themselves their meanings. Their significance is realized in the formal qualities of the work. These qualities have been described by various scholars as "truth," "expressiveness," "communication," and "significant form." Thus, the work of art puts demands on both the creator and perceiver of the art object, which go beyond the more obvious dimension of the literal content. The demand on the perceiver can be explained as a cognitive device which consists of sensing, perceiving, and conceiving— even beyond the immediate and formal properties of a work of art. For example, a child viewing a representational painting like Grant Wood's *American Gothic* would first attend to the obvious subject matter of the painting. Then he would view the color, line, value, volume, etc. This in turn may stimulate his perception of a particular meaning or intuition which sensitizes or enlightens his appreciation of the painting. This could be a new experience which is personal and beyond the artist's intention. In *American Gothic* a child might recall some feelings about farms or the somber quality of the two central characters that were not a part of the artist's design.

In teaching art appreciation in the elementary grades it is important for the teacher to recognize that insights obtained by children are not arbitrary ends in themselves. Rather, they are unique experiences that can be renewed and expanded in the process of art appreciation. In this light it can be seen that art appreciation is part of the humanistic attributes of education.

Art Education Curriculum

The arts can profitably employ systematic methods in the formulation of the curriculum of art education, in teacher training, and in the teaching of art. This section will deal with the development of the conceptual structure of the art curriculum.

At this juncture it is appropriate to discuss briefly the dominant characteristics of the art experience that must be recognized and utilized by those responsible for the formulation of the elementary art curriculum. The ineffectiveness of much of our elementary art education in the past has been the inability of art educators, curriculum makers, and teachers to recognize and understand the patterns of artistic development that are essential in bringing to fruition the inherent individual ability of all children.

It is important to differentiate the external structure conceptualized by the curriculum maker and the teacher as being separate in degree from the individual internalized experience of the child. The external conceptualized structure of the art curriculum should be a developmental guide to expand the child's aesthetic experience, kinesthetic development, social awareness, and self-evaluation.

One of the qualities necessary to a dynamic art curriculum is the preparation for the development of those aspects of education called aesthetics. Aesthetic awareness (or the old word, "appreciation," with a new connotation of active involvement) is being sought after through aesthetic education. One necessary factor in developing this is the task of encouraging teachers and students to establish a dialogue with the work of art, that is, to discuss openly the work of art in the student's own terms, according to his personal experiences and perceptions. In reality, a good work of art has all the immediate qualities necessary for appreciation on a personal level.

The development of aesthetic awareness is undeniably an important objective of the elementary art curriculum. However, the aesthetic experience should not be approached in a strictly academic manner; it should be taught in the context of the complete artistic response of the young student. The art instructor should encourage children to search beyond the depiction of factual expression by informing them of design principles in a manner that is on their level of comprehension. For example, children in the first and second grades can be imaginatively shown the basic potentials of many kinds of art materials. They can be taught to identify and use basic colors, to express simple values and intensities, to explore the relationships of basic color combinations, and to be aware of a great multitude of tactile qualities, both in the art media and in natural and manufactured objects.

The elementary art curriculum should stress basic art principles in every grade even though this may at times appear repetitious. It is this concept of repetition of art fundamentals that gives structure, articulation, and meaning to the art program. Consequently, the developing child will be more responsive to aesthetic growth, more attuned to plastic exploration, and more aware of the language of art.

Children as they enter kindergarten and the first grade bring with them elastic internalized experiences of a limited kind. Their aesthetic experiences have been to a great degree dependent and shaped by a depth of personal intensity encountered in the environment of their homes and communities. The child's artistic responses in the early primary grades, reflecting the nuances of their world, are usually wonderfully fresh and disarmingly naive.

In today's elementary art programs, there is a trend toward presenting relationships between the art form and art activities. The art experience, whether from the point of view of the creator or the perceiver, is undeniably personal and distinct. In the primary grades, aspects of aesthetic criteria cannot be taught academically, but must be elicited by the individual child according to his depth of experience. Therefore, attempts to teach color as an abstract phenomenon apart from the actual activity of painting, or to teach the fundamentals of composition as a distinct exercise of artistic judgment, are usually not recommended.

To maximize the educational potential of all students it is necessary for the teacher of elementary art to establish realistic objectives. Well-planned objectives are the necessary fuel to sustain and enrich the art programs and to provide the means for evaluation. However, it is extremely important to attempt to gauge the climate of one's class before structuring objectives. Objectives, of course, exist for student growth and development and not for teacher expediency.

The following objectives, which were noted in the introduction, are presented in the ideal and should not be considered as absolute or conclusive: (1) to introduce art as a visual language; (2) to help develop and exercise student's perceptual capacities; (3) to introduce students to man's cultural heritage; (4) to develop personal aesthetic and critical

awareness; (5) to help students achieve personal and cultural identity; (6) to develop skills in art commensurate with their abilities; and, (7) to foster the creative potential in every student.

It has been noted earlier that as we progress further into the anesthetized society of automation, the stimulating influence of art will be a more critical factor. Thus, the importance of developing a good art program in the elementary schools and surrounding communities cannot be overemphasized. On the other hand it is optimistic to think that an exciting and vital school and community art program can help negate the prevalent distinterest in thoughtful artistic community planning and redevelopment, roadside environmental landscaping, and, most important, the development of a deep and lasting personal commitment to the arts.

Art should serve in a greater role as one of the cultural bridges to understanding contemporary international problems. Much of children's art the world over needs little translation. This form of visual communication has great appeal to children and is a factor that needs more study as a contributing element to the total educational program. UNESCO and the International Junior Red Cross are two organizations that can be utilized in exchanging children's art.

Today, an art education is mandatory in a society that manufactures a plethora of consumer goods of questionable taste and produces a veritable fountain of art products of varying quality. It can justifiably be said that man's innate personality is not complete unless he has been aesthetically educated. The art experience kindles and sensitizes man's love of beauty and allows him to focus on the quality of design in consumer goods, and most important, reject the shoddy and poorly designed. Aesthetic growth in the general public could have the salutory effect of forcing industry to re-tool.

Traditionally art educators have been exploiting the problem-solving characteristics of art as a learning device. Art methods are currently being used in the entire educational program to stimulate learning in almost all phases of the curriculum. For example, the abstract concepts of mathematics are being graphically illustrated and solved through the constructing of models of buildings, architectural forms, and abstract sculptural forms, using such simple materials as string, straws, toothpicks, paper, and cardboard. Also, children can design and construct intriguing string sculptures that visually illustrate problems in geometry. It is amply evident, then, that the uniqueness of art with its mortarlike characteristics can help cement the seemingly unrelated disciplines into a rational whole.

In an age of increasing conformity, one of the last refuges of individuality resides in the symbolic processes of art. The art curriculum, therefore, is essential as a means of providing the catalyst necessary to continue this never-ending search for the expression of visually artistic nonverbal communication. It is a misconception to think that children's art, or in fact any art, must express some kind of standard, publicly accepted set of symbols. The importance of adhering to the personal nature of individual symbolism is becoming a more significant aim in the field. For example, many thoughtful school curriculum guides stress at the beginning of their philosophical introductions that true art expression is based on personal experience that is uniquely and idiosyncratically the student's own.

It is an all too common fault for adults to guide children's art into patterns of representation that express the stereotyped conception of art. This can only suppress the child's normal expressive tendencies. It is difficult for people to accept the fact that "art cannot create anything but its own symbolic forms, and these forms are not symbols of any external ideas, but of the artist's own intuitions, feelings, and fantasies."[1]

Within the context of a creative art program are the necessary mental and physical responses of problem-solving, assimilating, manipulating, forming, and evaluating visual configurations through the use of many materials and tools. Besides the traditional materials of elementary art, new and exotic materials such as plastics, glass, and metal derivatives are opening up new and exciting worlds of visual and tactile exploration.

It is necessary at this point to discuss further the bases, stated briefly in the introduction, for including art in the curriculum. First of all, art can be justified in our society as an inextricable sinew of our lives based on an understanding and appreciation of historical traditions of the past and cultural demands of today. Second, it is the schools' absolute responsibility to insist that *all* children receive an education through art. Art should not be the special province of the talented, or the laboratory of therapy for the maladjusted, but should be offered to all children as a natural vehicle of expression. Third, schools, in conjunction with local communities, must carefully evaluate their children's artistic needs in light of social responsibility. The artistic needs of the culturally deprived child will undoubtedly necessitate a different degree of emphasis than those of the upper-middle-class child. Fourth, the hierarchy of administration having the initial responsibility of sanctioning and structuring the external characteristics of the art program must permit the classroom teacher and the student the final decision in expressing their individual internal needs. Fifth, the foundation of the art program must encompass the sociological and psychological needs and interests of the students, and must utilize the educationist's knowledge of growth and development, perception and creativity.

[1] Herbert Read, "The Realist Heresy," *7 Arts #2,* ed. by Fernando Puma (New York: Permabooks, 1954) , p. 30.

The sixth and final point to be considered is the means and methods of placing art into the matrix of the total elementary educational program, without losing its identity. If art is looked upon as the natural unfolding of creative endeavor, and as the mortar necessary for constructing the interrelationships of many disciplines, then there should be little difficulty in finding "time" for it during the school day. In this respect, art ceases to be an activity, isolated from the realities of the "hard" disciplines. The possibilities for using art expression both in its own right and as a means of learning other disciplines are endless. Considering that the entire elementary school program is predicated on preparing children to meet the demands and responsibilities of society, an art curriculum, conceptually designed and implemented by art supervisors and classroom teachers, can successfully energize the entire elementary school curriculum.

Correlation with Other Subjects

Today, one of the many difficulties facing the curriculum coordinator of the elementary school program is the often painful decisions on what subject matter is to be included in a program that is already bursting at the seams. Pressures from national, state, and local groups for inclusion of varied disciplines are becoming more and more powerful and difficult to resist. Unfortunately, as recent NEA surveys point out, the so-called "frills" (a usual category for art) are in many communities being forced from an already barren and uncreative elementary curriculum.

Though time is short, it is hoped that legislators, educators, and parents will realize that science divorced from the arts transforms our society into an inhuman instrument. Yet there are hopeful signs on the distant horizon, which portend trends of increasing enlightenment toward bridging the chasm separating the two realms of art and science. Recent studies relating to the concept of the structure of knowledge have shown striking similarities in many of the working processes of the artist and scientist.

Another trend of increasing importance is the new technical developments in instructional media. To the art teacher they bring entirely new equipment and materials and suggest new ways of using traditional art materials such as blackboards, charts, prints, slides, and films. The challenge to the art teacher will be the manner in which these new technical developments will be used in promoting and enlarging the art experience of the student. Instructional media can be a tremendous tool in developing correlation with other subjects or it can become a mechanical crutch readily used by uncreative, timid teachers.

Because art has immediate intrinsic appeal to most children, and because it can infuse other disciplines with symbolic structure and aesthetically pleasing form, it can serve as the visual structure for learning in all disciplines.

The Media and Tools of Art

Most young children are naturally inquisitive and capable of great ingenuity. Even the casual observer will notice how the most commonplace objects can fascinate children for great periods of time. Generally speaking, these play periods take place without direct parental guidance. One may logically ask if these periods of free play and exploration have creative longevity? We can safely surmise that this depends on the individual child's personal receptivity to perceptual stimuli and his as yet undefined, nascent degree of aesthetic awareness.

The child's objects of play or the artistic media of expression need a residual force of personality and kinesthetic action to extract an aesthetic response and awareness. And furthermore, aesthetic longevity is dependent on the quality and quantity of the child's artistic response.

Ideally, it is in the classroom, under the direction of a trained and sympathetic art teacher, that the child's artistic development can be given the impetus for the proper foundation and continuity. The teacher trained in art education can help insure that the child's artistic journey is neither a tailor-made easy success nor a frustrating failure, but is so structured that the strategic raw materials of art can provide the necessary individual stimulation for continued artistic growth.

The media and tools of art must first of all be considered as a means of illustrating individual expression and not as an end in itself. In other words, art media by itself is no guarantee of a successful art program. The art specialist and the classroom teacher must adapt the art media and the resultant techniques to fit the external and internal growth patterns of the child. In order to accomplish this task successfully, they should be aware of the developmental stages of children's growth, should understand the unfolding of the creative process, and should have knowledge of the foundations of art education.

Many elementary classroom teachers have had little or no training in art, and without the special services of an art consultant are hesitant about introducing art into their classroom work. The teacher can partially compensate for this lack of training by selecting professionally recommended instructional media such as audio-visual materials, art education magazines, journals, and books on art techniques, art education, and art history. It is relatively easy to procure this information from many sources in the community. Next, the teacher should make every effort to become familiar with basic art media and their uses for particular age groups. She should experiment by using these materials in sequentially planned units.

It has been pointed out that unsupervised children's play with commonplace objects has great natural appeal to children. This is exploration related to direct experience, but it is not necessarily aesthetically cumulative. The very young child needs the structure of planned perceptual education, in art as much as in reading or mathematics. It is important also to recognize that art cannot and should not always be the handmaiden of other disciplines. Art perpetually wedded to utility can be unnecessarily restrictive and dull for young children. Therefore the classroom teacher should understand the importance of the art process as a natural phenomenon of stimulation and exploration utilizing the children's perception; definite time should be set aside for nonspecific excursions into the fantasy and excitement offered by the glow of liquid colors, the tactile appeal of variegated surfaces, and the intrigue and adventure of illustrating one's daydreams.

A word of caution is necessary at this point. Teachers should be aware of the pitfall of constantly relying on the so-called "happy accidents" of art. Globs, smears, and careless strokes can be mistakenly judged by the teacher as remarkable achievements. Of course there are times when this does happen, but the child is quick to sense false evaluation. Aesthetic evocative experiences are usually the result of the child's working, sensing, feeling, and assimilating his media, and not through ephemeral experiences.

This reservoir of experimental play can now serve as the perceptual building blocks necessary for the more formal instruction in the processes of the art experience. In this next stage of aesthetic development the child can cognitively expedite the uses and potential of his art media. And as he matures, his domination over the media and tools increases, permitting him to experience a greater depth of experience and facility of artistic expression.

The teacher should present a conceptually balanced art program that utilizes art choices throughout the semester. This would allow for proper sequential offerings. It is wise to have a sufficient selection of projects and materials so that the children can freely experiment, with the assurance of finding compatibility with a particular media and project. Obviously, too many projects can be as frustrating as too few.

Occasionally the classroom teacher should turn from the traditional art media of crayons, paints, and paper to the "environmental art materials" of nature (vegetables, gourds, fruits, leaves, weeds, bark, wood, stone, rock, etc.) and the "environmental materials" of man, generally classified as "manufactured leftovers" (scrap metals, wire, beads, buttons, scrap lumber, tiles, linoleum, plastics, etc.). These materials offer plentiful opportunities for spacial, sculptural, and tactile exploration.

When planning for the purchase of art materials, the classroom teacher should consider the following points. (1) The materials should be "children's size." That is, they should be keyed to the average age level of the group: crayons should be large enough for easy manipulation, scissors should have blunt ends, and powdered poster paints are preferred to the less practical liquid variety. (2) Approved art furniture, adequate physical space, and cleanup facilities should be provided. (3) The teacher must continually emphasize the dangers inherent in the careless use of tools, materials, and solvents, and stress the safe, proper use and care of the materials.

THE STUDENT

Child Growth and Curriculum Articulation

The development of children's art has both fascinated and puzzled scholars, art educators, and psychologists for many years. Indeed, authorities have been engaged in a constant debate concerning such questions as what the psychological sources and motivations of children's art expression are, whether there is aesthetic merit in their art, whether there is a definite developmental sequence to their drawings, and if there is some universality of artistic expression common to most young children.

Art expression in all age groups is a personal and socially conditioned evocation of certain visual qualities that draw upon a complicated array of varying psychological and sociological factors. Each individual's artistic expression is a uniquely personal testament that reflects (in various degrees of clarity and intensity) some of the many facets of his personality, behavior, perception, and intelligence. Yet, in spite of these personal characteristics, certain commonalities do appear in much of children's art throughout the world.

There is much argument today concerning the validity of attempting to structure a developmental sequence that can be correlated with such factors as chronological and mental age. Also, there is much dispute revolving around the question of whether children's artistic expression can be characterized by general types or aptitudes. There is agreement that the child's unique personality is of greater significance than his conformity to a group. Some authorities are convinced that it is all too convenient to tabulate and categorize children's art according to salient

characteristics and similarities. To do so would blind a teacher's awareness of the nature of individual expression, they believe, and would thus cause teachers to view their student's art expression according to very limited concepts; this could lead to their forcing a conformity of standards, causing the student to feel extremely restricted.

On the other hand, some authorities think it necessary to define children's art into very broad, elastic categories of expression. However, within this concept, they believe the teacher should understand that children's artistic characteristics cannot be limited or directed to a particular age group because of each child's physiological, psychological, and sociological uniqueness.

Although the attempt at classifying children's art according to developmental sequence is far from settled, it is abundantly clear that each child's art expression is the product of his own particular qualities and experiences in life. It is also clear that children tend to pass from one stage of artistic development to another.

Investigators into children's art have identified three broad sequences or stages of development. These stages are not to be construed as absolute or rigid classifications, but only as a scaffolding containing known visual characteristics that can be placed over the living continuum of children's artistic expression in order to better understand and identify these characteristics. The three phases have been validated through empirical and descriptive research, which has established a correlation between developmental stages and age scales, and has shown that these stages are generally the same for most children.

The first developmental stage has been variously called scribbling and manipulative. It usually occurs between the ages of two and five. It is characterized by what at first appears to be uncontrolled scribbles or scratchings, as if the child is reacting to the stimulus of the art media with his entire being and without thinking. It is not too uncommon for the child to respond to his drawings and paintings with unabashed emotional expressions.

As the children draw and paint they usually verbally accompany their activities by singing, talking, expressing fear, anger, surprise. They seem to enjoy thoroughly the actual physical manipulation that is afforded by the media they are using. It also appears that children at this stage have little desire for closure; they seem to enjoy the production or "doing," and seem less to care about or understand the meaning of achievement or completion.

As they progress in this stage, their drawings become more controlled and exhibit rhythmical patterns of large sweeping and curved lines. Soon primitive figures and representations of objects, such as animals, houses, and airplanes begin to be evolved.

**ANDERSON COLLEGE
LIBRARY
ANDERSON, INDIANA**

79249

When the child enters kindergarten, the introduction of new art materials can produce a degree of clumsiness—the degree will depend on prior learning, musculatory strength, coordination, and the ability to make cognitive discriminations concerning various concepts. The rate of development will vary enormously from child to child and the teacher must be aware of these individual differences.

The second stage of the child's development in art, usually occurring between four and eight, is generally labeled the symbolic stage. This phase is marked by a greater development of the child's musculatory strength and coordination, and a greater expansion of his conceptual faculties which enables him to define and organize pictorial details.

The children's scratches and scribbles are now evolving into primitive, though extremely personal, descriptions of their known world. Circles of all sizes now become transformed into the sun (complete with radiating lines), the moon, and heads. Now heads acquire crude characterizations by suggestions of eyes, nose, and mouth. Animation appears when the heads sprout lines for arms and legs. Soon peripheral symbols appear in drawings and paintings. There are indications of size, of movement and speed, flight, texture; and later sky and ground lines make their appearance.

It is important for the classroom teacher to understand that this process demands of the child a greater differentiation and organization of detail, but that it also demands a greater amalgamation or fusion of both the cognitive and residual or noncognitive processes that generate the child's aesthetic and artistic development.

The process of fusion can occur at any time during this stage and is a remarkable advancement for the child because this is the first time in his life that he is using a conscious symbolic form of visual communication. Now patterns or schema become formalized, with the child developing his own unique symbolic methods of expression. This change can usually be detected in kindergarten.

A further outgrowth of this process will be the depiction of more than one symbol in the drawing or painting. This is a more sophisticated advance into thematic relationships which can illustrate to the child a means of bridging the differences between fantasy and reality and which helps him to understand the connection between his environment and his symbolic evocation. Essentially, this is the same involvement the mature artist becomes aware of.

One of the major difficulties in building an effective art program in the elementary grades, especially during this critical period of early symbolic development, revolves about the attitude of the classroom teacher. As has been earlier noted, the majority of elementary teachers have had little or no education in art. Consequently, their approaches to art education may vary from sincere and worthy efforts to complete indifference or, worse, misapplied and injurious programs that can cause creative atrophy. The latter influence is in part responsible for propagating the adult mania for visual conformity, in that the child must fashion art forms "suitable" to the taste of adults.

It must be stressed again that in earlier stages children draw more of what they feel than what they see.) Their art development is a series of steps that builds a conceptual rationale toward visual maturity. It is within these steps that conflict often occurs between what the child does and what the adult thinks he should do. Children represent their visual images in a much simpler manner and these representations are commensurate with their physical and psychological conditioning. It is harmful to, indirectly or directly, channel children's art forms toward clichés.

It has been noted earlier that young children can best develop their artistic abilities under optimum conditions. These conditions, unfortunately, are many times negated by sincere but uninformed adults who know little of the meaning of the creative process and have meager knowledge of the importance of individual differences that is especially appropriate to children's art. A case in point is the mania that some adults have for neatness and conformity when teaching children's art.

Children at this stage of development generally exhibit an uninhibited and sometimes explosive manner in dealing with art media. Their drawings and paintings represent a thrilling adventure in the exploration of new colors, lines, forms, and textures. To the average adult who has been conditioned to accept rigid visual configurations, the unreconstituted forms of children's art are at times thought of as chaotic. In order to make the drawings and paintings more meaningful to the adults, methods have been developed that attempt to insure pictorial neatness, legibility, and definable progress so necessary in evaluation. These well-known methods include the stencil of concise figures, duplicated teachers' drawings in which the children are admonished to color "within the lines," the copying and tracing of trite seasonal motifs, and other unimaginative techniques, which are guaranteed to instill conditioned conformity and timidity of expression.

As the child progresses through the later phase of symbolic expression, he includes in his art, peripheral or thematic relationships. This attention to related concepts and the expression of greater differentiation of detail is a great step forward for the child in understanding relationships to his environment. A further development of this phase is the use of the familiar ground and sky line. To children, the ground line is generally a line of reference on which other symbols may have a kind of child's justification for existence. The ground line may take many forms.

It may be a drawn or painted line on which are situated various forms, such as symbols of people, animals, trains, cars, buildings, etc. It also may be curved to illustrate hills, mountains, rivers, and roads. Or it may be multiple lines on which many of the above symbols are placed.

A few more characteristics of this stage should be noted. Children at this age are usually egocentric and this quality is at times vividly expressed in their drawings and paintings. For example, it is not unusual for children to draw themselves much larger than their peers. Also, children boldly exaggerate sizes of objects as these objects are felt in importance. A policeman's arm may be extremely long in relation to the rest of his body. To the child, this may express certain emotional qualities associated with policemen. And, it is not too uncommon for children to illustrate dominant personalities, such as their parents, older brothers and sisters, and their teachers as extremely large individuals, who at times dwarf their surroundings.

Children are amazingly inventive at this age. They utilize intricate cognitive processes in solving visual problems of great complexity. Some children will illustrate extended periods of time by utilizing sequential movement in their drawings and paintings. In this particular form of expression the child may depict himself many times moving from one point to another. Children will also illustrate simultaneous interior and exterior scenes, sometimes called X-ray drawings.

As the child progresses visually, in coordinating the world of reality to his personal means of expression, color becomes less of an abstract fantasy and more of an associative adjunct to reality. The child's color range becomes commensurate with his visual perception, and therefore much of the charm of freshness of his art is lost.

Within the continuum of child development, the third and final general phase that can be definitely categorized is called "beginning or dawning realism" or "the preadolescent stage." This phase generally occurs in the nine to twelve age groups and roughly approximates grades 3 to 7. The beginning of this phase may be marked by great enthusiasm toward fanciful expression in most media of art. However, depending on the unique personal characteristics of the child, and the classroom atmosphere, certain changes are evident in the over-all expressive qualities of the art. The children now become aware of sex differentiation, they begin to acquire a feeling toward social problems which minimizes their egocentric behavior, and they soon learn that they are held responsible for the consequences of their actions.

Also, at this phase, many children become painfully aware of their seeming inability to express visually symbolic forms in a world that demands literalness as one criterion of artistic success. Consequently, a child can become hesitant and unsure of his artistic abilities. He will

strive for over-elaboration of detail in order to compensate for what he feels is a lag between his abilities and what he sees and is taught to be visually correct. He will strive for definite depiction of detail in portraiture, clothing, and landscapes. Unfortunately, this literal elaboration is often accomplished at the cost of aesthetic qualities.

Design elements are sometimes neglected and the child may become so overly aware of shading and texturing techniques that the desired compositional elements of the drawing or painting are lost. It is not unusual to see children manipulate color in the same manner as they manipulate patterns of light and dark values. They begin to experiment in shades and tints in order to capture the reality of local color inherent in the subject that they are painting.

Paralleling the child's concern for color is his attention to pictorial space. Through individual experimentation and knowledgeable instruction the child learns to illustrate distance in his drawings and paintings by employing the devices of simple linear perspective, and overlapping forms and atmospheric perspective.

In summation, the following characteristics can be attributed in a very general way to the third phase of child's art:

1. The processes of cognition now begin to help develop a greater awareness of pictorial reality.
2. The child begins to search and experiment with newer and more relevant symbolic characterizations which will start to approximate visual reality.
3. The child begins pictorially to develop space, distance, and relative size in his drawings and paintings.
4. The child begins to experiment with values, shades, tints, modeling, and texturing.
5. There is at times a disproportionate emphasis on detail.
6. The child now begins to associate subject matter preference with his sex.

The child in our particular culture during this phase is passing through a crucial period in his development. He is leaving his personal world of uninhibited symbolic depiction, where playful action and artistic expression are synonymous, to one of measured reality which is determined not by himself but by adults. However, through sympathetic and understanding teachers, children can bridge the gap of visual insecurity and begin to develop positive artistic qualities of design commensurate with their individual abilities.

There has been little curriculum articulation through the grades in elementary art education in the past. Because many teachers are unsure of the processes of individual artistic development as it relates to child growth, their programs have varied from highly structured and deliberate approaches to completely unstructured situations. But today art educators are reviewing the teaching and learning conditions associated with planned art programs. The consensus of past experiences indicated that many teachers of elementary art felt that deliberate training in art would over-intellectualize the act of creativity and too severely cramp the child's perceptual growth. Formal training in art processes was and still is thought to be justifiable only for secondary and professional art students, and totally unjustified for elementary school children. However, the deliberate art program can, by utilizing the child's cognitive learning processes, exercise discrimination, develop judgmental values, and be creatively expansive if constant individual and group evaluation is practiced.

An example of this process can be seen in the planning of a field trip. The teacher discusses with her class the nature of their visit and perhaps introduces slides, films, or other relevant educational aides. Depending on the teacher's estimate of available time and desired intensity of study, it might be appropriate for the children to sketch scenes of interest to them at the site. When the children have returned to class, group discussions with one another and the teacher during the act of painting, and after the painting is completed, can have strong positive effects in expanding and unfolding the child's conceptualization of the creative act.

Art as a spontaneous activity has long been an accustomed mode of presentation. Too often, as has been mentioned, it can be license for chaos under the guise of "exploration." An experienced and sensitive teacher, however, can help develop a dynamic art program by knowing when the spontaneous processes should be instituted. This calls for propitious flexibility of approach—a knowing when this aspect should be implemented, for whom it should be implemented, and how it should be implemented.

To a great extent, spontaneous implementation exercises the child's precognitive learning and defines his emotional set. It helps to objectify his subconscious thoughts, and graphically illustrates his established behavioral patterns. The carefully planned art program and the judiciously paced spontaneous art process are both important learning situations built around the needs and interests of children. Consequently, these vital elements in the structure of art, if wisely employed, can help lessen the many hours spent on repetitious, time-consuming, and meaningless activities often labeled as art. A meaningful art program would provide for vertical articulation (logical curricula relationship from lower to upper grades) without the fear of overlapping previously learned activities, because art would not be taught as a means of covering an unending series of projects within a specified time, but would be based on the criterion of maximum individual development, regardless of the process, media, or technique used.

The Psychological Base of Children's Art

The young child and, to a certain extent, the mature artist generally are not consciously aware of the creative process that enables them to produce works of art, which makes for difficulty in defining what is meant by the aesthetic process.

The psychology of art has been one of the most baffling and most neglected of all the branches of psychological research. Contributors to the study have been quite varied in their orientation toward art—they have been anthropologists, philosophers, aestheticians, practitioners of psychoanalysis, psychologists of different schools, art educators, art critics, and artists.

From this growing complex of divergent approaches have come opinions, theories, and research that are controversial, and sometimes findings that are inconsistent with established scientific methods. Too often, studies are not based on systematic observation or rigorous empirical research, but on individual biases, which at times only perpetuate anachronistic philosophy or misinterpreted psychological principles.

Moreover, theories of art have been very difficult to formulate. Recent investigators in the psychology of art think that a theory of art must ultimately include factors relating to cognition, perception and affect, and feeling.

Art educators, in discussing the psychological motivation for children's art, believe that drawing is an innate extension of children's personalities. Children's drawings have been described by many as a natural language of communication and expression. However, psychologists have taken great pains to attempt to define the specifics of the processes of forming an art product. In this regard, they have made numerous studies which have investigated the manner in which the child sees, feels, and reacts to various visual stimuli, and his means of replicating these stimuli through drawings.

Art educators and elementary teachers, in order to have a more effective influence upon administrative policy in designing the art curriculum, should be aware of a number of areas of concentration in the study of the psychology of art. Though the following survey is by no means complete, it does offer art education some fruitful areas for consideration.

1. Most contemporary students of the learning process feel that though the processes of thinking are very complex, learning itself is simple. Yet at this time there have been no general laws promulgated which can characterize its methods.

2. Many of the current theories of behaviorism, though scientifically feasible in the laboratory (where isolated instances have been defined) are not at this time readily transferable to the very intricate behavior of daily classroom performances. However, there is great promise in the utilization of some of the behavioral concepts of learning that have been applied to technology. The most publicized of these are the teaching machines.

3. There is evidence today that seems to indicate that the introduction of a certain amount of ambiguity in the educational program would facilitate learning. A degree of flexibility in the interpretation of art can help to achieve a creative program.

4. Recent developments in the theory of cognition have supplied a number of interesting and useful approaches toward a theory of the psychology of art. Within a developmental framework, these include the essential ideas of perception, concept formation, and the yielding of a theory of intelligence as an evolved structure. This theory has been advanced by Piaget. His studies concerning schemas (that is, the child's mastery of spacial concepts) and the fusion of vision and other sensory modes are potentially of great value to art education.

5. Art education is necessarily concerned with nonverbal materials. Though research in art education has focused much attention on the processes of personality development, it should consider the aspects of cognitive and symbolic content. Therefore, any theoretical construct in art education utilizing the cognitive mode in learning should incorporate the processes of affect and its effect on the intellectual as well as the personality structures.

6. The development of human behavior is exceedingly complex and occurs in sequence, which requires time for its development. Consequently, the classroom teacher must be aware of and responsive to children's individual needs. It is the researcher's responsibility to persuade the teacher that the well-learned concepts of adults, which we take for granted as intuitive, have been acquired over long periods of time. This has been illustrated by Piaget's studies in the intuitive ideas of space, time, number, and causality. For the child, awareness of these concepts comes through continuous experiencing and experimentation with objects existing in the everyday environment. In Piaget's theory the child's concept of space supports the idea that the child's visual symbols are intimately tied into his conceptual growth. Thus, these studies suggest that children should be given perceptual activities as aids in fostering

the development of a concept of space. This suggests that young children be given art media that would facilitate detailed spacial exploration and expression. For example, children may use ball point pens, finely pointed flo-pens, and pencils to visually describe still life, contour drawing, landscapes, etc. Therefore, it may be advisable for art educators to design the curriculum on the concrete rather than on the abstract.

7. Recent psychological research has indicated that children and adults have creative ability and aesthetic sensitivity commensurate with other potentials. With this assumption in mind, it is interesting to note that deprivation of sensory and perceptual experience in the early formative years would possibly retard or permanently limit the development of the child's cognitive structures, and thus severely inhibit later creative potential and aesthetic sensitivity. Therefore, it is incumbent for art educators, in the development of new curricula, to develop learning situations that are rich in visual stimulation.

Whatever theories of art are developed, it will always be necessary for the individual teacher to guide the process. Art education has been correct in insisting that art is a unique attribute of the human condition and that ambiguity is a necessary ingredient to induce and foster creativity. Art education should devote more attention to the function of the teacher as a stimulus to the creative process, and the varied use of media as catalytic agents in the creative act.

Evaluation

An extremely difficult task in art, for both the teacher and the student, is that of evaluation. The attempts to establish external criteria and standards of achievement are often prone to failure and frustration. A review of recent literature indicates that one of the basic causes of contention in accepting a method of evaluation lies in the willingness of the teacher to accept the individual philosophy of the person who constructed it. This acceptance aggravates what teachers feel is the uniqueness of their approach to teaching art. That is, by accepting and utilizing criteria not of their own making they give implicit recognition to external standards for evaluating their students.

In art, the teacher must make continuous decisions concerning evaluation based on the individual child, on the broader aspects of the art curriculum, and on the total educational program of the school. The teacher at best can make only relatively short-term appraisals of student work, and this is generally limited to observation of progress within the classroom environment.

Evaluation is an exceedingly complex process, which must logically begin with the formulation of objectives. This also involves deciding how to obtain evidence on how these objectives are achieved. The second step is to ask the question, "How are the processes of interpretation used

to understand the meaning of this evidence?" The third step is to make judgments about the strengths and weaknesses of individual students. The process is complete when decisions concerning desired changes are made in regard to the curriculum and to teaching.

Within this definition of evaluation, the art curriculum is involved in the entire educational process. Therefore, the following evaluative procedures can be developed: first, identifying important educational objectives, which would be stated in terms of desired student behavior rather than in terms of teacher-directed behavior; second, planning for a wide range of student-centered experiences needed to obtain these objectives; third, developing a sympathetic rapport and empathetic understanding of student desires, abilities, and weaknesses so that appropriate experiences for eliciting positive behavioral attitudes can be designed; fourth, utilizing the procedures of evaluation to determine the qualities of personal artistic development in order to assess the degree to which pupils obtain these objectives.

Even though the production of and the appreciation of art is extremely individualistic and subjective, this does not mean that appropriate objectives cannot be formulated and generally adhered to. The development of appreciation and taste and the techniques of building artistic skills should be related to the mainstream of artistic tradition. This does not imply that the art curriculum must be bound by the restricted dogma of conventionality. Individual artistic growth can best develop when there are clearly defined objectives consonant with the best of traditional and contemporary models.

Clearly defined objectives do not preclude flexibility in the art curriculum. The art teacher must be ever alert to capitalize on the unexpected turn of events which are very frequent in the art program. During an art activity a student may accidentally stumble on a unique situation which may be far removed from the original intent of the project. It is in situations such as this that the teacher must exercise creative judgment in order to evaluate this new approach while redirecting the student toward possible new and more satisfying personal artistic fulfillment.

In art, evaluation becomes part of the creative process through the impetus of instruction, the student activities of learning which involve selecting, discriminating, organizing, and synthesizing. These activities must be evaluated on an individual basis and not according to arbitrarily defined group standards of achievement.

This leads to one of the most difficult decisions to make in the art program, which is the assignment of grades. Assigned grades can instill in the child who does not excel in art a feeling of futility and docility toward his own personal development; and the child who does excel may be shunted off to work on his own, leaving the greatest teaching effort in the amorphous grouping labeled "average." In this manner, the teacher's concerns are directed toward educationally unsubstantiated groupings that in reality do not reflect the individual artistic abilities of all students.

Another pitfall to be avoided in evaluation is that of basing grading on developmental sequences of children; these are nothing more than broad generalizations that loosely characterize groupings of children according to types or aptitudes of artistic expression. The concept of developmental sequence is unfortunately used as a grading device in the mistaken belief that children will neatly fit into a statistical form.

The child's art expression is the unique product of his particular qualities and experiences in life, and therefore each is significantly different from all other children. Consequently, instruction in art should be in the forefront of educational evaluation by encouraging the uniqueness of the individual's artistic development.

The child can be more thoroughly evaluated according to longitudinal development. One way this may be accomplished is by keeping portfolios of the children's art work from the beginning to the end of the instructional period. In this manner, the child would have the opportunity to witness the growth and development of his art work, and he would be able to measure his own progress over a period of time.

Complementing this would be frequent consultations with the teacher regarding the child's feelings and experiences in the art process. This can be further expanded by encouraging the student to write descriptions of his thoughts concerning his art work. This process can be extremely enlightening by revealing attitudes toward his art work and allowing him to describe his feelings of inadequacy, if they exist.

Through these procedures, the concept of encouraging the child to develop according to his particular abilities is greatly facilitated. Evaluation will therefore be the measure of the growth of the individual child and not be based on external criteria. Finally, attention will be focused first on the process of artistic development, that is, the creative process as experienced by the child, and secondarily on the techniques of execution, which are less important. Grading, if necessary, can therefore be honestly based on individual growth, which is the most important contribution the art curriculum can make to the general development of the child.

THE TEACHER AND OTHER STAFF MEMBERS

The Classroom Teacher

In the elementary school there are several systems under which art is taught. At present the most common is the multi-subject or the self-contained classroom, where the general classroom teacher is responsible for teaching all subjects, including art. There is now a trend toward the grade school teacher's teaching only one or two subjects, as the junior high and high school teacher do. Art, therefore, would be taught by a teacher with special training in art.

Whether a teacher is responsible for all or for a few subjects, there are qualities that a teacher of art must possess in order to do a good job. Unfortunately, the classroom teacher cannot be expected to be as effective as the art specialist. The problem of upgrading the quality of classroom art teaching can be met (1) by teacher-education institutions that should provide sufficient units in studio art and art education training courses; (2) by the school district's careful teacher recruitment and hiring practices; (3) by professional in-service art courses provided by school districts and colleges; (4) by an enlightened school administration which can provide an adequate budget, proper materials, and guidance; and (5) by encouraging a development of a more culturally mature public.

The ability and commitment of a teacher of art can range from the completely unprepared and disinterested generalist teacher, to the interested teacher with training as an art minor or major, to the dedicated artist-teacher who is both a practicing artist and a committed and capable teacher. It does not always follow that the latter will be the best art teacher, but such is usually the case. Whether giving full or part time to teaching art, whether trained fully or partially, the teacher of art should know and love art, should be proficient in it, and should be able to relate the teaching of art to child development. Of course these same attributes apply to other subjects; but, teaching ability is even more critical in art since it is less structured than a more arbitrary subject. The elementary classroom teacher must have many capabilities. She is responsible for teaching all subjects throughout a long and usually difficult day, and she has the further responsibility of developing mature social behavior. For art instruction the teacher is responsible for supplies, scope, and sequence of the art program (unless she has help from art guides and art supervisors). She must be an unusual kind of factory manager. Timing for a structured subject like arithmetic is easier to predict than for an art lesson.

Art is a searching time where the final answers are at first unknown and sought after. Ideally in art, though impossible within the present system of mass education, an open-end time period should be available since one is not able to predict when the final answer or final perfection will be achieved. The classroom teacher, therefore, must either provide for more flexible use of time and subject matter or provide techniques for individualized work time. Two practical approaches to this problem are to have an "art table" in the classroom where students can take turns completing their work, or to have art as a homework subject.

The Resource Teacher and the Consultant

There have been a variety of systems for providing the teaching of art by someone more specialized than the classroom teacher. These systems have included the special art teacher, the art consultant, the art supervisor, and team teaching arrangements. A trend is gaining momentum toward a more specialized system of teaching subject matter. The high school and junior high school system of teaching seems to be moving down from the sixth through the fourth grades. The pressures to restructure subject matter and teaching techniques in science, mathematics, and foreign language have been largely responsible for this. Unfortunately, in many schools throughout the country, the effect has been to squeeze art partially or totally out of the program in the elementary and junior high school.

If the idea of team teaching becomes widely accepted, and many elementary school principals predict that it will, there will be need for a wide range of instructional talent. How such programs will work out over the years in actual practice remains to be seen, but team teaching seems to many the answer to the question of how to attract more of the ablest college students into elementary school teaching. The opportunity for a teacher to take advantage of her special field of interest is exciting.

It seems likely that the self-contained classroom will continue to be the most common pattern in the kindergarten and the first three grades. Grades 4, 5, and 6 will probably be taught more and more by art specialists. If there is no junior high or intermediate school in a district, the seventh and eighth grades will also be involved in this changing pattern. Unless there are tightly constructed administrative plans for team teaching, additional staff will need to be employed. The problem of additional staffing, causing additional economic strain on local districts, points up the growing need for increased financing of education from national funds.

Ideally, the teacher of art should be a most creative person. The emphasis in education has been on the academic and technical. Without exception, writers in the field of art education feel that the teacher is the most important element in an art education program. There is some, but surprisingly little, disagreement as to what some of the qualifications are for a good teacher of art. The kind of teacher that should go into art teaching is one who can cope with the pedagogical methods of imparting knowledge, who has a sense of the place of art and education in society, who can guide without being overbearing, who has a capacity for being interested in several students' approaches at the same time, and who has the ability to verbalize clearly. The teacher's personal art practice should be continued; artist-teachers have the advantage of being searching, productive individuals.

Unlike the teaching fields of science and mathematics, art teaching positions are not in abundance. There are many people who have the qualities desirable for teaching art but they must, in addition, really want to teach. It is difficult to be both a good artist and a good teacher. The professional artist does not need to verbalize; he meets his work with flexibility whether in oil or stone in his attempt to bring order out of chance. In a classroom for some it is not possible to maintain a creative or even an uninspired order. The problems of timing, of diverting oneself to several students rather than concentrating on one work of art at a time, are sometimes frustrating and confusing to some artists.

As good as a teacher might be, it is a mistake for the teacher of art to isolate herself into her classroom. Some teachers plead for this right, arguing that it gives them individual vigor not to be bothered by the many demands that can be made upon the art teachers. This argument is a good one if the demands of holiday decorations, posters for every contest, and the multiplicity of instant commercial-like school art is forced upon the art teacher. Her class can become a studio factory that has little educational meaning. If a reasonable amount of school requests would allow for quality this could provide a worthy motivation.

Compared to the sciences, the art field has been slow in attempting to revitalize its teaching. Designing the structure of the subject, introducing more visual aid material, and improving classroom facilities all will help, but no single factor is as important as improving the quality of the teacher. Increasing the number of specialists in art would go far in improving the profession.

An elementary school district can get a start in the direction of greater excellence with a minimum addition of staff budget by hiring an art consultant, either on a part-time or full-time basis. One art consultant can spark new interest in art and guide the teaching of art in the elementary schools of the district. An art consultant can offer the following services: demonstration teaching, helping to structure lessons, helping to write an art guide, conducting in-service art classes, helping with school or district art exhibits, consulting with teachers who need special help, helping with bulletin boards, and working with special groups like the physically handicapped or the academically handicapped. Left to an overburdened general supervisor or left to chance, the art program is bound to suffer. To fill this kind of position requires special qualifications: experience as a classroom teacher for at least two years, a talent for organizing, knowledge of a wide range of art activities with the ability to teach these to children or teachers, an ability to be forceful and tactful, and an ability to foster enthusiasm and confidence in others. There are also usually special certification requirements, which vary with different districts and states. Whatever the position in art education, the requirements are not easy to meet and the standards should be high. These standards should fit the specialist art teacher in the elementary and secondary schools as well as the college teacher. If anything, good teaching is more crucial on the elementary school level since it will set the tone for the future. As far down as nursery school and kindergarten, a sound start in art has a good base in the children's natural verve and artistic potential.

The Principal and Superintendent

The classroom or special art teacher cannot do the job alone. The principal is the key person in the chain of command.

Compared to high-priority subjects like reading and science, art needs support and design even to hold its own. Children will tell you that art is important to them and the very young will demonstrate that art indeed is a natural visual language, but it is the school administrator who must be convinced of this. There is often a sorry lack of communication between the teacher of art and the administration. This is sometimes understandable since each represents a different point of view. In order to develop the best art education program, the combined team of teacher, principal, and superintendent must ask and solve questions dealing with philosophical concepts and operational problems in the art program.

Programmed Instruction

Even the most ardent advocate of programmed instruction admits that the most important element in teaching is the teacher. The machine in programmed instruction is itself ultimately dependent upon man: man designed it, programmed it, and evaluated the results. No matter how many unique responses might be made by a machine, it will never be able to create and never be able to think. This by no means rules out the use of programmed instruction. Art might be the last subject matter frontier, but, just as audio-visual equipment is an invaluable aid to the art teacher, there are areas in the teaching of art where machines will be very useful. Many teachers of art feel threatened and fight off any attempts at using machines in a systematized way. This is probably a natural battle for the art-centered person to wage, but whenever the machine can release the teacher for worthwhile pursuits and whenever this can be coupled with achievement on a higher level, the practice should be undertaken. Given the teacher's present role, there is no danger that "the machine will take over." The central problem is, in what area and exactly how might programmed instruction be used to advantage.

In the teaching of art, compared to science, there is more individuality in methods. For this reason a standardized course of study and stereotyped uses of equipment would never be universally accepted; the use of programmed instruction will be an individual matter.

> . . . a logically valid answer will depend partly upon the value commitment of the art educator—what his educational goal is—and partly upon the tested consequences of machine vs. human teaching.[2]

Even if the art educator is not temperamentally adapted to the use of machines, technological development might make it so tempting in the future that art teachers will make greater use of them. At present, however, even the motion picture and slide projector are rarely used by many art teachers. This makes for a lack in the program since there is an increasing number of good quality films and slides available. To see an original work of art of any real worth is a rare experience for most students. Even if an occasional field trip is possible, a slide preview and follow-up would increase the educational worth of the direct experience. The accumulation of knowledge in the field of art history and contemporary art is overwhelming even to the specialist. The organization and systematization of some of this material can be aided by a wise use of programmed instruction. In reality, the main problem is that the profusion of knowledge simply proliferates, making the process of individual selection a difficult task.

Art is a visual manifestation of the immense capacity of man's emotion and intellect; therefore, the art teacher has great responsibility to unfold some of this cultural heritage as well as to provide means in the art laboratory for student growth. Programmed instruction wisely used can help provide lessons and tests in art history; display art that relates to the individual or group laboratory work; show examples of reproductions of art that correlate with other curriculum subjects; present technical information to help with problems being encountered in art; and so on. Existing programmed instruction machines are not being used to capacity, and there are machines yet to be invented and developed. This potential should be seriously considered by art educators. Since machines are usually programmed and designed for such skills as reading and mathematics, attention is needed to use machines that primarily involve the projection of visual images. The field is unlimited, and we must be receptive to changing tools in the future.

2David W. Ecker, "Teaching Machines and Aesthetic Values," in *Studies in Art Education* (Washington, D.C.: National Art Education Association, 1961), p. 15.

There are strong and creative voices like Marshall McLuhan and Buckminster Fuller, who, though not directly involved in the field of art education, say that we must understand our technology and learn to design it for man's good. Art education also says this. Design, a word that is often used in art, is widely used in the broader society. To design is to compose—to suit to a purpose. A basic aim in the teaching of art is to develop within students the capacity to understand the purposes and products of design in society and design as they practice it in an art laboratory. Design, whether intuitive or analytical, is a basic element of art and is also fundamental to art education. The various disciplines, more often than not, are working their separate ways. Architecture, art, art education, programmed instruction are in isolated compartments. In the foreseeable future these separate efforts should be combined toward solving human problems.

Teacher Training

There has always been controversy over the kind and extent of teacher training in elementary art education. Doctors and carpenters evolved to their skill and professional behavior after years of formal and informal training. If the ultimate context of teaching children is not built into the training methods, courses in art and art education will be of little consequence. The internship system of training general elementary and special art teachers offers a minimum amount of pre-teaching courses and attempts to get the student into teaching as soon as possible. Most of the courses are in-service in nature. The success of such programs is dependent upon a very careful screening program. Only the mature and highly capable are given a chance. The problem, in general, is with effective screening devices. Most programs depend upon multiple interviews, college grades, work records, and letters of recommendation. This system of learning on the job often finds initial placement of interns difficult.

There has been a long-evolving tendency for colleges not to be purely teacher-training colleges, but for teacher training to be part of a liberal arts college. Through the years a wider college participation in teacher training and educational research has become evident. The wider college assumes much or all of the training in the four-year Bachelor of Arts program. The education department takes over for a fifth year. Whatever system the states and colleges follow, the education departments have lost some of their dominance.

The present danger is that too great an influence will fall in the hands of subject specialists and laymen, who are not aware of educational complexities. The advocates of subject matter emphasis hope that the personal involvement of the college student will be at a higher level, and that the subject matter taught to elementary classes will be more challenging. The educational methodologists argue that knowing the nature of learning and being able to translate subject matter and to motivate is the prime problem. The encouraging thing about the present public interest in education is that an improvement in subject matter and material support of education should be forthcoming.

Whatever the system of teacher training, whatever the emphasis in the methodology controversy, the student-teaching aspect of teacher training is of prime importance. However, before the student teacher is ready to do practice teaching in an art class, a certain number of college courses and classroom observation are usually required. These should be administered by the education department or subject area departments in the college. Art and art education should also be a basic part of the general elementary teacher's training, since she will be teaching art and will be using much art in general teaching; "specially trained art teachers" will more than likely not be available to the beginning teacher in elementary school.

The college program is usually so crowded that all above recommendations cannot be required and met. But the teaching of art needs to be improved and expanded, and a key place to start is at the teacher-training level. At least at a very minimum the general classroom teacher should have had a wide offering of studio art classes, decorative arts, art history, and art education courses.

During the student-teaching period in the general elementary classroom, the master teacher should be responsible for two major phases of the student teacher's training. First, he should oversee the student teacher's training in general classroom management. This would include familiarizing the student with the general aims and objectives of the course of study, and the complexities of general classroom management. The second phase would concentrate on the specific procedures inherent in the art program. Among the particulars to be learned would be the artful use of lettering, the design and execution of displays and bulletin boards, and the proper procedure for organizing demonstrations of classroom projects. The knowledge of the subject matter, art, and the ability to communicate as a visual language should be basic necessities to even the generalist in education. Art is a basic language for children entering the schools and certainly should also be for the teachers entering the profession. Children, of course, are the prime subjects in education, and teacher training should never forget this. Student teaching is valuable because only in a contextual and dynamic situation can a student learn to guide and teach art to children.

The student teacher must assiduously develop a positive working relationship with her class. She must quickly gain their confidence by evidencing an expertise in the complexities of classroom management, by expressing knowledge and understanding of student affairs, by having mature dealings with other adults, and finally, by showing a genuine enthusiasm and critical ability in art.

Most of this advice applies to teaching in any subject matter area. The eternal problem is that art is only one of many subjects that must be considered by the general classroom teacher. Both teacher-training and regular classroom programs often slight art because there is not enough time to cover all the subject matters. Experience has shown that the employment of special art teachers and art consultants will improve the quality of the teaching of art in the elementary schools, in addition to improving pre-service and in-service training.

The art specialist should have a major in art, as well as training and experience in the teaching of art and other subjects to elementary school children. More specifically, the training of the prospective teacher must include the studio performance, the study and practice of art education, and the study of art history and the humanities. In practice there is a certain amount of general agreement in the curricula of college training for art teachers, but a wide variation of specific requirements unfortunately exists, as it does for the general classroom teacher. In any event, whatever the balance, training and experience in the subject matter and in the process of teaching art is essential for either the general classroom teacher or the special art teacher.

THE CLASSROOM, THE SCHOOL, AND THE WIDER ENVIRONMENT

The Classroom

Even with the best teacher, education within a poor schoolroom would be able to go only part way. This is especially true in the teaching of art, since it is a subject that requires the use of special equipment by the teacher and every student.

Just as there are two main teaching systems in the elementary schools, there are two main classroom systems—the self-contained classroom and the specialized classroom. In grades K to 6 the self-contained classroom is most common, where art, as well as all the other subjects, is taught. In the case of the specialized classroom, where the children move from room to room, the art room has special art equipment and a special art teacher. This is the system used in the junior high schools (grades 7

to 9), intermediate schools (8 to 9), and, probably in the future, in the fourth grade and up.

Many teachers prefer a multi-subject classroom, which gives them greater flexibility of timing and coordination of subject matter. The self-contained classroom also has the advantage of being less expensive since more subjects can be taught to more pupils; however, with the increasing interest in improving the instruction of subject matter, more special teachers and special classrooms are called for. Especially in the upper grades there is a need for special art classrooms. This will come about by improvising as best as possible within the existing classrooms and, preferably, by designing new classrooms for special use in the teaching of art.

With the use of special art teachers there is still controversy as to whether it is better for the teacher to travel from one classroom to another or for the children to travel to the special art class. Taking everything into consideration it is better to have a teacher working in a special art classroom. But no matter which classroom system is used, certain basic facilities and equipment are called for and flexibility of use is desirable. Designing the new and making use of the old require a great deal of practical thinking and the combined efforts of the teacher and the administrator guided by the literature in the field.

The following basic needs should be considered for a classroom where art will be taught:

1. *Storage space* is a prime necessity for art materials and for work in progress. Shelves, wall cabinets, space under tables, and other space are called for in quantity. In some cases doubling up on function can be economical. For example, the front of a wall cabinet could be used as display space.

2. *Work space* is essential for individual and group work. Desks and tables provide the usual work surface, but there are times when large work can best be done on the floor or on a wall surface. In the self-contained classroom in particular, individual desks are preferable to a few large table desks that must be shared by several children. Although it is good to have large uninterrupted surfaces for art work, it is preferable to have a few tables and be able to have individual desks. The individual desk has the advantages of providing for individualized, concentrated work, while allowing for combinations of desk arrangements offering flexibility of surface area and many possibilities for student grouping. Each desk can contain basic art materials and the student's work in progress. The main requirement for the desk is that the surface be uninterrupted and that the top surface be a rectangle without curved corners.

3. *Display space* is needed for the exhibit of students' work, for demonstration material, and as a special area for the projection of slide

and motion picture materials. Architects and the school staff need to work closely on the practical as well as aesthetic designs. Wall surfaces should be made of a material or have a covering that is easily washable and is able to receive changing exhibit material without damage. The past tendency toward the overabundant use of windows in school architecture is now giving way to the use of less window space on lower walls, to allow for more useable wall space and more controllable light.

4. *A water supply area* in the classroom and a lavatory close by is essential to an art program. Sinks should be provided with heavy-duty traps. There are still many classrooms that do not have sinks and those are a challenge to the teacher's ingenuity to improvise with carrying devices.

5. *Other needs* depend upon the nature of the art program. In the self-contained classroom an art center is advisable. This can be in the form of a table or a wall desk providing a "cafeteria" center for the distribution of materials to other work areas. Or it could be a work area which students take turns using, either as part of or in addition to the regular art class. Special activities like ceramics or crafts might require a separate section of the classroom or an additional room.

The specific use of a given classroom depends on the particular teacher and children that will use the room. The classroom will usually outlast the service of a given teacher and it is impossible to predict the nature of the children and kind of art activity that a classroom will see in the next twenty years. For this reason it would be a mistake to be rigidly specific in the designing of a classroom. The approach should be humanistic and functional.

The School

The design of schools has improved during the last ten years. Architectural planning is based more and more upon a combination of function and aesthetics. Preliminary planning should be a joint venture so that the architect becomes aware of the variety of intended uses, but literal thinking should not hamper the architect's aesthetic quest. It must never be forgotten that children have an intuitive appreciation of their surroundings and the architecture that will be their home for the day. As a matter of fact a good working principle in school architectural planning is to provide space for murals, mosaics, and creative landscape that will be executed by the children themselves as part of the art program. Pride in creating a suitable and aesthetic environment is a basic aim of the best art programs.

Even for the general planning of a school, an art teacher should be on the planning committee. If the stage of planning has preceded the staffing, as it usually does, the services of an art supervisor or even of an artist should be sought. In the early planning stages even extreme ideas should be encouraged. Flexible thinking should reach out for creative solutions. Eventually all ideas should be tested for their practicality by involving as many of the community groups as is educationally feasible. A good start would be a meeting of representatives to discuss tentative plans with the architect. Special art projects and the display of art or correlated material allow art to reach beyond the classroom into the hallway walls, the library, the lunchrooms, and the auditorium. In the upper grades part of the art program could operate a kind of decorative art agency to prepare and install displays and exhibits throughout the school. The art teacher is the key to this and the school should provide suitable space for exhibits and displays throughout the building.

A growing trend in elementary education (as well as the other grade levels) is to utilize existing school plants for a greater part of the calendar year. There is also a tendency now to have a greater variety of activities in the school building. In some cases adult education and nursery school education are combined with the elementary program. Here again flexibility in architectural planning can adapt to these changing demands.

The Wider Environment

Just as a nation cannot shut itself off from the world, so a school is part of a wider community. There have always been casual ties, but the school and its wider environment are becoming increasingly interdependent on both formal and informal levels. The community beyond the school boundaries has much to offer the elementary students but the educators in charge must be selective. The school must make a continued conscientious effort to guide its students in the wise use of their environment. Television, radio, museums, and libraries should be considered sometime-partners in the educative process. Efforts should be made to influence these institutions to work with the art program. Even if the school has a good collection of art slides, reproductions and motion pictures, for example, there is no substitute for field trips to a museum or gallery to see original work.

For decades population movements were toward the urban centers and now the trend has been reversing itself. New kinds of satellite communities are developing that are close enough to urban centers of work but often too far from the city's cultural opportunities. Availability of nearby land and speed of transportation are compensating factors that can make satellite cultural centers more possible. The expatriates from the cities are beginning to realize that a complete life demands more than a bedroom community can now offer. The more progressive communities are building centers for the performing arts and are encouraging the growth of civic art galleries and the development of adult facilities for the participating arts. Elementary schools in such communities should be provided with a rich cultural base.

As automation gives more leisure time to the adult world, children should learn the value of art as both a participant and observer so that their present and future lives can have more meaning. The very young child has the least amount of trouble knowing what to do with his leisure time. He accepts the language of art as natural and important. The school and community have a mandate to nurture the potential of their children.

CHAPTER THREE

ART AND CREATIVITY

Art education has been vitally concerned with creativity for
the last several decades. Without the creative process as a
central concern the subject of art is transformed to a lesser
skill and achievement. It is not surprising that the competition
in scientific achievement and in economic markets has de-
manded the talents of the ingenious. Moreover, the skilled,
even the brilliant worker is not enough. Early research—both
in science by Guilford of the University of Southern California,
and in art education by the late Victor Lowenfeld—aimed at
finding factors in creativity that could be measured like I.Q.
Independent of each other their preliminary findings were
quite similar in spite of the differences in their fields. Research is also drawing fields like anthropology and even science
closer to the goals of art education. There is an increasing
similarity in the writings of science education and art education—both in language and in educational aims. A psychologist, Jerome Bruner (who has been a dominant influence upon
science education), values "intuitive thinking"[3] as do many art
educators, while art educators are also becoming concerned
with the value of "cognitive thinking."

The process of intuitive thinking is common to both art
and science, but in art intuition is relied on to a greater extent
and for a longer period of time. Problem-solving is more
personal in art and does not have to find proof in the measure-
able world. Common to both fields is the search for significant
relationships or connectiveness, as Bruner states. World history,

[3]*The Process of Education* (New York: Vintage Books, 1960), p. 13.

science, and art have been intimately interrelated. However, contemporary history has shown that technological expedience allied with science can destroy aesthetic values and consequently atrophy basic life-nourishing values. As an example, Lewis Mumford and John Ruskin, despite their historical separation, have both agreed that whenever the architect surrenders to the engineer he perverts the sculptural form of architecture into a functionalism that loses the human scale and becomes a rigid academism.

In some societies conformity is high, but in our own society degrees of individuality are more possible than ever before in man's history. In the professional realm of art there are innumerable styles and individualized extremes. As with the mispractice of Dewey's philosophy of education, there is often a mispractice of the implications of contemporary art. Often one mechanistic trick lesson after another is used as a series of novel levers toward manifesting creativity. This quest for novelty for novelty's sake usually leads toward permissive restlessness. However, on the other hand, art education in the late nineteenth century disdained creativity for the mechanistic formulae of rote and conformity. This graphically expressed America's preoccupation with the negative aspects of Victorian industrialization, and likewise had a negative effect on art education. We need an art education that is related to the best values of our present day life.

Universal education is an ambitious but basic commitment of our democracy. Even though the goal is toward educating everybody there should also be a goal of educating the total person. In overemphasizing certain subject matter the curriculum generally leans toward materialistic practicability. The ideal should be a liberal arts core which includes the arts. This would be a more ideal foundation for the elaboration of special adaptive skills and job training.

That everyone is educatable and that creativity is a practicable catalyst for a higher level of learning have been emphasized by writers in various fields. Preschool children do not need to be taught art. The language of art loses out as children grow older, and by adulthood they can become visual illiterates. In the upper grades especially, the excitement and the skills of art cannot be left to chance. The creative process should not be eliminated from education. The laboratory is the best vehicle for inducing creativity.

Though art should not be the only path for creative exercise it certainly should not be a minor or forgotten part of the total curriculum. Art in its own right and in correlation with other subjects might well take the exalted position as nerve center of the curriculum.

ART AND THE ARTIST

In education there is a healthy trend toward seeking answers in curriculum development and teaching method beyond the classroom, by observing the accomplishments and habits of outstanding people in the field. In art, for example, quotations of artists and psychological studies of the process of creation are beginning to become an influential part of research which should be stimulating to art teaching in the future.

> I am not here to reflect the surface (a photographic plate can do that), but must look within. I reflect the innermost heart. My human faces are truer than real ones.[4]

The artist Paul Klee, in a sophisticated vein, is describing not only his work and the work of other artists, but also the work of very young children and the work of older children who have had at least an adequate art education. The teacher and the school should take note of the philosophy of looking beneath photographic exteriors. Creative achievement is not easy to come by even for artists themselves. Moreover, it is not child's play, though children's art has similarities to the work of their older counterparts and there are elements of play in both. Concrete definitions of both word and plastic form illustrating our most basic preoccupations—love and personal philosophy—generally elude us. Therefore, art cannot be similar to all people at all times; consequently in art education "... the very subject being taught operates against our attempts to reach agreement about precise methodology for the teaching of art."[5]

It is far easier to teach a precise subject in a precise way than to teach art. There are many guidelines and the subject matter itself is exciting and unique. The very lack of precision of ultimate destination makes pioneers of the artist, the teacher, and the student. Perfection is in the image of inner necessity rather than under outward dictates. Rannells believes that the creative process "itself is a continual action and interaction between the artist and his art. . . . His commitment is total; nothing less than this can be enough."[6]

Complete commitment cannot and should not be the aim of art for every child in the elementary school. The basic purpose of art education is not to train professional artists. The other extreme, however, of inane

4Paul Klee, *The Thinking Eye* (New York: George Wittenborn, Inc., 1961), p. 20.
5Jerome Hausman, "Elephants, Blind Men, and the World in Which We Live: An Editorial," *Studies in Art Education*, N.A.E.A., Fall, 1960, p. 4.
6Edward W. Rannells, "Thoughts on the High School Art Program," *School Review*, Autumn, 1964, p. 357.

play can beat a path away from art and away from education. Many artists actually are inspired by the honest work of children. Picasso, Miro, and many other artists find direct inspiration from children's work. And, in turn, children, if given a chance, do find inspiration from artists' work. Teachers could find guidelines and inspiration in the self-evident parallels in the way both children and artists work.

Art has been an age-old preoccupation, in primitive tribes and in sophisticated nations. Research has suggested for some time that high rates of crime and psychological breakdown would be curtailed if individuals could find greater meaning in their existence. Psychoanalysts and therapists have found that intuitive language and art are a direct bridge for therapy. Making a distinction between fiction and nonfiction is within the capability of most people; severe confusion of the two worlds is often the sign of the insane. Art is neither objective reality nor is it fantasy. Art as substitute for the world is kept in the proper perspective by a frame. Either the producer or consumer can participate in the play or ritual of art (the half-way point) and is thereby armored against falling a victim of complete illusion. Not only the process of creativity, but also the subject matter of our art heritage and contemporary art, should be more fully utilized in the curriculum.

THE STUDENT AS CREATOR

Individual differences and differences of age level are more apparent in children's art work than in any other curriculum area. If art teaching has a proper setting with good materials and guidance, then the transition from art as a natural language to art as a well-tutored language will be successfully made. If it does not, the natural ability will atrophy and the high school, college, and adult student will have lost the language of art. As children grow older they are aware of their surroundings in a more realistic way; but by this time they should have learned more sophisticated uses of art materials and have learned various ways of stating art forms in terms of their age levels. More often than not, immature art is an embarrassment to both student and teacher, and avoidance or rejection is their usual (but wrong) response. Just as in the teaching of reading and language arts, so in the teaching of art individual differences in children must be met.

Formal education generally divides children into groups by age and sometimes by certain abilities. Whether the teaching of art is done by the classroom teacher or by a special art teacher, individual differences and age levels will be readily apparent and good teaching should be conducted on these terms.

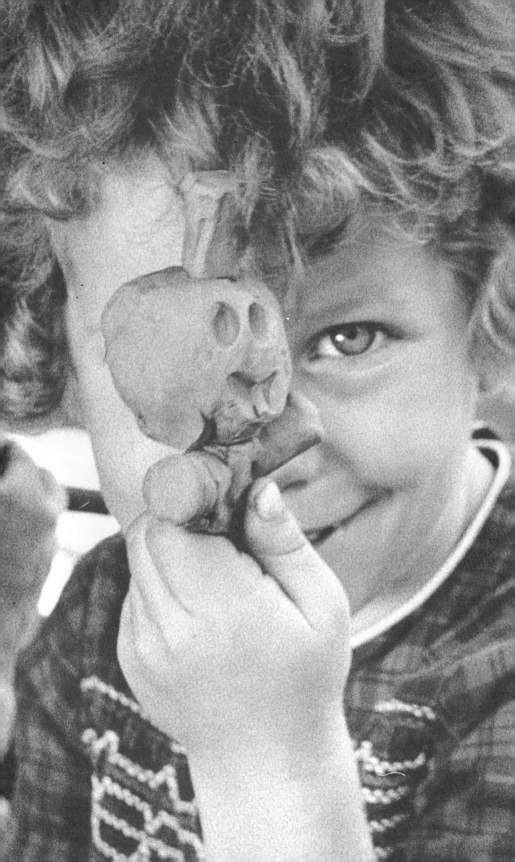

Whether by an artist or under tribal ritual or by a child, the purpose and act of producing art have much in common. Whether the work is primitive or is objectively analytical—whatever the style or frame of reference—the producer's conscious or subconscious purpose and the limitation of the art materials will dictate the form.

Today the teaching of science attempts to make much use of techniques of discovery and problem solving. In art these are the basic ingredients of the creative process. More should be made of teaching strategies in art that will encourage this kind of activity.

Discovery in science must eventually seek for the final answer in the outside world. Discovery in art is an inner-world search for truth and rightness. This search for the right form and arrangement must be an individual one in art. The fact that there is no one truth should be a primary tenet in any enlightened art class, but there is an inherent danger of permissiveness. A good teacher with sensitivity and taste will be able to guide the activities properly. Children are not able to verbalize the psychology behind the creative process; but, using their basic drives and their own world of experience as levers, they have a good intuitive base for their art work.

When children are immersed in art activity it is difficult to divert them. Motivation is more of a problem as children get older. Distractions increase, conformity strengthens its grip, and the realization that art is not a major concern of our society makes itself known. For a child to be motivated many things must be overcome. Play no longer operates as carefreely as before and work loses its contextual roots. Involvement is the key. Even the best teacher needs time to set the mood. Sometimes a matter of weeks is needed before a working atmosphere is achieved where there is a group will toward commitment.

A purposeful creative act is more than random play. This often must be guided as well as motivated. The staging of conditions is the responsibility of the teacher. It is easier when the temper for creativity has been fostered rather than left to chance.

THE DYNAMICS OF CREATIVE TEACHING

Creativity must be cultivated. In observing a very young child painting with great joy and confidence one might conclude that creativity springs eternal, and that art teaching would not be necessary. At this early stage no guidance at all is better than tampering, which could be destructive. But this stage does not last long. As children grow older more of the teacher's craft and knowledge are necessary. Everyone has differing degrees of creative potential. Suppression can be imposed at an early age.

The stage must be set and the cues carefully weighted in favor of creative confidence rather than repetitive conformity. Use rather than misuse of creative energy must be a guiding principle of good teaching.

Of course the teacher must be creative, must be perceptive in finding and seeking out creativity in the students. The teacher must be committed to the art of teaching art. However, being overzealous in teaching can be debilitating and will yield negative results..

Some art teachers are artists as well. The artist-teacher can be an unusually successful teacher. Such a teacher must, however, be able to verbalize about the nonverbal language of art and must be able to guide others as well as himself. She must be able to gear the creative process to the age level and the abilities and interests of the students at hand.

In the fields of science and mathematics teachers are learning how to systematize the teaching of subject matter and to start the sequence of the unfolding of skills and knowledge at lower grade levels. Art as a kind of creative laboratory work does not lend itself to this method of systematization. One thing that the art teacher can learn from the new methods of teaching the sciences, however, is that the strategy of discovery and individual pursuit of problem-solving is preferable to persistent reliance on the static teaching techniques. But the problems of scope and sequence in art need much consideration and revision. For example, the laboratory method of teaching art, if handled poorly as far as organization and teaching are concerned, is apt to suggest to children an invitation for chaotic behavior. Another problem exists where the beginning teacher expects unrealistic performances in art. Searching and struggling for perfection, in terms of oneself, is the basic aim of the art process.

Depending upon its objectives, an art lesson can be presented formally or informally. If formal, the lesson can be presented to the entire class, to a section of the class, or to an individual. Demonstration and any information regarding materials and techniques usually should precede the motivation of the lesson so that, fired up, the students can launch directly into their work.

There are many plans and systems suitable for classroom organization. For example, in an informal approach, each child can have materials at his desk available for a given project or to use when the occasion arises. There can be a wide selection of art materials in the classroom, for all to use at any time, or a monitor system can be used to dispense materials. A work table can provide art materials and a setting for work to be done at any time. This latter system is especially adaptable to the self-contained classroom.

Whether the formal or the informal method of presentation is used, art demands an open-ended work time. Both the project and the artist's personality make for wide variations in the time needed to turn in a finished work. It takes special planning to overcome the compartmentalized time packages found in mass education, but there are many ways to allow for the completion of work. A teacher, for example, can allow an unfinished work to go home for completion. If plenty of time is available in a given lesson there will usually be some students who will finish early and will be able to move into work of their choice or start another prescribed project; or, a special work center can be provided where turns can be taken for the completion of work.

When the children have launched into their work it is better for the teacher to err on the side of noninterference than to be overbearing. At the outset she should make it clear that help will be given only when needed and asked for. If the lesson has been well presented there should not be too many questions. The laboratory tradition of individual persistence should have been well established. There are many ways to help, depending on the individual need. The teacher can ask pointed questions; she can provide a piece of scratch paper for the child to work out the problem; she can sketch out several solutions (never drawing directly on the student's paper and never suggesting the specific solution); she can suggest that the student consult a picture file (just as reference material is used in the language arts). At the discretion of the teacher, a question or solution of any one child can be transmitted to the entire class so that all might learn. Adults and upper-grade children alike are timid about pioneering. Students as well as artists face a difficult trial during the creative process. While the lesson is in progress, the teacher needs to be encouraging and supportive, especially during the initial period of searching. This does not imply that there should be leniency in accepting unworthy efforts. The teacher is primarily a guide in helping the student expedite the creative process. Teachers should always attempt to have their students do their own thinking and acting. Indeed, art on any level is a matter of individual and cultural determinism.

Most teachers in childhood lived in a world with less leisure per person than his students will have when they become adults. The process continues and is a miracle of technological advance; but, there are many perplexing problems that must be faced by educators, as well as all leaders in society. One of the problems is making the best use of leisure time.

Technological change has resulted in much population mobility. In addition to being confronted with problems of quick social change the teacher sometimes comes from a different racial and social background than the student. Special attention is therefore needed to bridge the gap of cultural commitments.

There is a tendency for some teachers to try simply to transport students into the teacher's own cultural orientation. To have children shift from working-class to middle-class standards is educationally unjustifiable. Art has many faces and can be the best language at hand for communication, at least at first encounter between the teacher and students. More than a simple language, art has the potential of allegorically solving problems that are real and pressing. Art is a means of solidifying the individual identity of students who have been challenged by social pressures.

More should be said about the specific art areas in teaching. For the ease of ready reference there follows an alphabetical listing of some art areas which are common to the elementary school, ranging from "Appreciation" to "Weaving." Much of the material in this section was developed by one of the authors (who was then art supervisor of Castro Valley School District) and art representatives from each of the twelve elementary schools.[7]

Appreciation

The main objectives in teaching art appreciation are to develop (1) aesthetic sensitivity and critical awareness and (2) conditions and skills necessary for creative participation. In its largest sense, to appreciate art is to be aware of one's own identity as it is related to past and present cultures. A related phase of this process is to develop knowledgeable children and adults who can make wise selections in the arts. The raw material for this is abundant and interrelated. It is man- or nature-made and varies in quality and quantity. It is found anywhere from a museum to a marketplace to an outpost in the jungle. With the environment an intermingling of both man-made and nature's products, it is impossible to dissociate the two. Both the influence of culture and the influence of nature work upon the painter. Without getting into the problem of heredity and environment in this section, let us limit our scope of nature to the exterior world of earth, sky, and living things. At every step, however, each individual will "see" and react to nature in terms of his cultural orientation. Nature influences the primitive who creates a rain god image, a child who draws a symbol of a happy sun, and the Oriental artist who is influenced by contemplating the location before he paints a landscape. The artistic byproduct can range from symbolic personification to romantic acceptance of nature. Any number

[7]Castro Valley School District, Mark Luca, editor, *Art Guide—Grades K-6* (Castro Valley, Calif., 1960), pp. 43–201.

of artists (or children) seeing the same sunset will paint as many different interpretations as there are interpretors.

The ability to appreciate art is not reserved for the highly educated, the rich, or even adults. Children are often more receptive than adults. The teacher has a definite responsibility to make art appreciation a working part of the total school program. Never before have there been so many resources available. Large reproductions of paintings (as low as a dollar) and popular magazines that often cover the arts are only two of the sources that bring this material within the reach of every teacher. However, relatively little material is available that is appropriate for grades K through 6. It is here that the teacher must draw upon her knowledge of her grade level, her background, and the availability of materials.

There are many teaching strategies that are possible for both individual and group study of art history. The following is a simple time-place structure for the study of art in a wider context, which can be designed by the teacher or by the students.

CONTINENT	COUNTRY	TIME				
		B.C.	A.D.	500	1000	today
North America						
South America						
Africa						
Europe						
Asia						

Art, Music, Literature, Anthropology, History, Drama, Architecture, etc..............

A single student can gain much from working at a solo study booth in the classroom or in a library or resource center. A classroom teacher with just a couple of pieces of audio-visual equipment and some organized resource materials—tapes, slides, transparencies, pictures—can bring in dimensions of enrichment that are rarely used in the classroom. Groups or the total class can use sound and projection as part of study programs in the form of "humanity dramas," puppet shows, or traveling-through-history teaching games—for example, a class-designed "program" on adventure and discovery with slides of paintings and photographs accompanied by appropriate tape-sounds of the times and narration by the students. With large refrigerator cardboard cartons painted white for a several-surfaced front-projection series of screens, or architect's tracing paper (or milky plastic) for rear-projection, the set-up can be inexpensive and can be adapted to the need of the learning situation.

On a larger scale children can help with an elaborate humanities light show where a visual and audio immersion is possible. With several pieces of audio-visual equipment that are common to the school (slide projector, motion picture projector, overhead projector, tape recorder, etc.) and with materials that can be obtained directly or prepared by the children (35 mm. slides, felt pen drawings on old 16 mm. motion picture film, tape recordings, and creative use of flashlights) you have the raw material for a "show" that can be exciting as well as educational. Education must serve the television generation, which is a very sophisticated one having been exposed to hundreds of hours of sight and sound. This exposure, unfortunately, has lacked quality and depth. Schools must offer quality and depth in audio-visual experiences, as they have in the past with selected books.

Wherever man's cultural remnants are found there is always some evidence that art was a very intimate part of his life. This is true of the cavemen as well as the sophisticated people living today. Through art we can relive moods and values found in both primitive and sophisticated art. In doing so we can add to our own cultural maturity. Through art we can share some of the universal desires of self-realization, security, adventure, wonder, discovery, and cultural identity.

Bulletin Boards

Bulletin boards, if successful, not only are effective educational tools but offer an aesthetic vitality to the classroom atmosphere. So that the children do not start the school year in a bare-walled classroom, the stage should be set with at least one bulletin board. Of course a certain amount of space should be left open and ready for the excitement of newness and change as the term progresses. The best aims of education and the nature of the children at hand should be of primary concern when evolving a bulletin board. There are times when a very traditional arrangement is called for, whereas for other purposes an adventurous approach is needed.

planning and creating a bulletin board

1. The teacher—either alone, with a group of children, or with the entire class—decides on a *theme* and a location for the bulletin board. Whether a large bulletin board or a small chart is used, the theme should be simple and yet challenging.

There are many subject matter and interest areas to draw from. The theme and its presentation are of course dependent upon the capabilities and interests of the children who will see the bulletin board. Following is a listing of areas with some suggestions of how they might lend themselves to bulletin board themes.

Arithmetic	—Games to strengthen skill in arithmetic, measurement concepts, time concepts.
Art	—Sequence processes like the making of a relief map or a mask; display of children's work or reproductions of paintings.
Calendar	—The year, the month, the day, with or without the inclusion of historical events, holidays, birthdays, folklore.
Classroom Business	—Monitors, representatives, plans for field trips, rules.
Current Events	—Local, national, or foreign news, or a concentration on a particular country.
Health	—Facts or rules; nutrition.
Holidays	—See section on *Holidays.*
Language Arts	—Coming events on TV or in the theater; books read or to be read; original poems or stories by the children.
Maps	—School, world, space, or a field trip to be taken; where children live, or where they spend vacations.
Music	—Display of art work done to music, the music and words of a song to be learned, photographs of instruments of the orchestra, appreciation.
Physical Education	—Exercise, sports and health, history of sports, Olympic Games.
Safety	—Traffic, at home, fire prevention.
Science	—Simple to complex machines, plants and animals, concepts.
Social Science	—Time charts, maps, transportation, nations.

2. *Guiding principles* are established. For example:
   a. Maintain a single, clear theme, statement, or purpose.
   b. The message should be legible and direct.
   c. All the details must be important, consistent, and related to the central theme. Discard the unnecessary. (There can be reference notations to see a certain book or picture.)
   d. The total design and all the elements should work as one. The design should be oriented toward the symmetrical or the asymmetrical. The style should be in keeping with educational aims of child guidance rather than copying poorly done commercial art.
3. The *collection of display and art materials* usually results in more than can be used. But before a bulletin board can proceed too far the materials should be at hand. The best source of materials is from

the children themselves—their writings, lettering, art work. Children can also be helpful in collecting pictures or realia, such as sea shells and leaves. The teacher's picture file, writing to sources, and loans from the library or the audio-visual department can often yield the key material.

Carving

Carving has been a limited art activity in the elementary school, since the use of carving tools is often dangerous and the materials used are often expensive. Both these factors can be overcome.

easily available carving materials: Wax (old crayons melted in double boiler and cast), soap, dry clay, and scrap lumber.

moderately expensive carving materials: (The following are carved as they are setting or soon after.) Plaster of Paris with sawdust or sifted sand or dirt, plaster of Paris alone or with coffee grounds.

more expensive materials: Carvocast (American Crayon Company); Zonolite (4 Zonolite plus 2 sand plus 2 cement; dry for 3 days); Magnesite (water is added to the dry substance to the consistency of dough); and foam glass.

carving implements: Sticks, scissors, spoons, paper clips, nails.

Casting

Unlike carving, casting depends on a mold that defines the shape. The mold (sand, plaster, wood, metal, cardboard) might be modeled (clay), carved, cut, or nailed, and wired or tied together with string. Plaster of Paris or casting plaster is the usual medium, but wax, Magnesite, Zonolite, or metals (usually done at a foundry) can be used. With plaster of Paris, designs are impressed in sand and objects inserted; when it is set the result is a mirror image casting which includes the inserted objects.

Chalk

Chalk is made up of pigment held together with pressure and binders. It has many uses in all grade levels. Chalk has the advantages of being readily usable with little or no equipment, inexpensive, compact, easy to store, and free from spoilage. Its disadvantages are that it is easily rubbed off, can be dusted onto clothes, and causes allergies in some children.

types of chalk:

1. *Colored chalk* comes in the common round sticks and the large lecturer's chalk.
2. *Blackboard chalk* is usually white limestone and, though harder in consistency, is sometimes used along with colored chalk.
3. *Pastels* are a finer and more expensive chalk, almost never used in the elementary school.
4. *Oil chalk,* like pastels is not used below junior high school level.

The following information refers only to the kind of colored chalk that is found in elementary schools.

surfaces: Blackboard, colored construction and poster paper, manila and white paper.

techniques:

1. *Used directly*—ends and side. With or without textures under the paper; rubbed with fingers, towel, or rag to produce blending and smoother effects.
2. *Used indirectly*—chalk dust rubbed on with fingers, cotton, or paper towel; on string which transfers the color; rubbed on the back (as a kind of carbon paper) of something like a map to be transferred; on a surface (like a leaf) to be printed; chalk dust floating on water is picked up with paper to give a marbleized effect.
3. *Used with a liquid*—applied on the surface, applied on the chalk, or applied with a brush, rag, etc., after the chalk is on the surface. The liquid can be water, liquid starch, canned milk, buttermilk, liquid soap, or diluted paste or glue (to milky consistency).
4. *Used with other media*—crayon, tempera, water color, pencil, ink yarn, collage.

activities and projects:

1. *Lettering*—break chalk to width of letter and use side.
2. *Maps*—rub chalk dust on, or outline directly and get careful gradation by rubbing.
3. *Murals*—on wrapping paper, or collage of separate parts.
4. *Drawings, illustrations, outdoor sketching.*
5. *Classroom decorations*—holiday decorations, border designs, bulletin boards, stencils.
6. *Crafts projects*—colored and decorated.

methods of protecting chalk drawings and projects:

1. By using such liquids as starch or glue along with the chalk; the work will be protected to a large extent.

2. By spraying with fixative (alcohol plus white shellac), clear lacquer, varnish, clear plastic, or glue plus water.
   Safety note: always spray outside of the classroom.
3. By covering surface with clear plastic, Saran Wrap, cellophane, or glass.

Classroom Decoration

A classroom should have the honest look of an attractive work center for a particular group of children of a given age. It should not look pretentious. It should look pleasant and well designed rather than dreary and cluttered. This is easier said than done where a number of individuals are responsible for a number of activities in a relatively small space. Therefore it is imperative that the teacher do planning before the children arrive and that throughout the school year the teacher and the students do more than minimum housekeeping. Some of the things to consider in a classroom designed and decorated for beauty and function are as follows:

unity. This can be achieved with a consistent color on the walls, a border design, an accent of color that appears in various places in the room. The arrangement of furniture and equipment for the best functional use will usually result in a unified floor design. Sometimes painting bulletin boards the same color as the wall, or making areas like the bulletin board and mouldings of a color different from the walls, will help tie the room together. A series of mounted pictures can rhythmically unify a room.

provision for main activity areas within the unity. Depending on the day-to-day program of your class the limitations of horizontal and vertical space should be designed with traffic lanes, areas of concentration (library corner, science table, etc.), and proper space for a permanent and a changing exhibit area and bulletin boards.

character of its own. As each classroom has a different teacher and set of children, a somewhat different atmosphere in each class is bound to result. This should be a natural outcome of serious purpose rather than a striving to be different for its own sake. Flower arrangements, murals, or the textile printing of a drape offer learning experiences while at the same time lending greater interest to the surroundings.

Clay

Clay is one of the oldest art materials used by man. It has been shaped into the most primitive utensils, and yet today ceramics are an important part of outer space rocket development. It is the best three-dimensional art material for grades K through 6. The stages of art development grow from the manipulative, to the symbolic, to the somewhat realistic. In the lower grades the finished product is not as important as is the working process; in the upper grades children have developed the interest and ability to do more finished and realistic work.

Following is an outline of the sequence that most clay lessons might take. Clay generally should stay within the limits of ¼ inch to 2 inches in thickness.

I. Obtain the clay.

Powder (clay flour)	Difficult to use. After mixing with water, clay should age.

or

Prepared (moist) white or buff or red	Comes in 25-pound plastic bags. If the clay has not been "pre-wedged" or pugged it must be wedged by cutting and smashing pieces together or by kneading. But most clay comes pre-wedged. Also, the clay should be the proper consistency.

TEST:
Not so wet that it sticks to the fingers (roll it over newspapers until dry enough) or not so dry that it cracks when bent (work water into clay).

II. Wet clay is worked into desired shape.	Each child can work at his seat or only one or a few children can work at a time at a work area.
A. Pinch or primitive method (K-6)	Children begin by making a ball of clay. Then it is worked into the desired shape without separating the clay.

1. Utensils
       or
    2. Animals and figures	

B. Coil method (5-6)
 	
    1. Utensils
       or
    2. Murals and figures
	Clay is flattened out with hand or rolled with rolling pin or cut with knife or wire and a circle is cut out of the clay with ice-cream sticks or scissors, etc. Coils or rolls of clay put one on top of another starting on top of the outer circumference of the circle of clay to form the walls of a jar, for example. To make figures, several coils can be put together. To join any two pieces of clay:
	Score (roughen with stick) and then
	Weld (wet surfaces with water or with "slip," which is water and clay) and work the edges together.

C. Slab Method — Same as coil method except that flat slabs are used in place of coils. The shape can be rounded or angular. Making a paper pattern first is a good idea.

D. Combination methods
E. Shaped over a core

III. Wet clay pieces can be textured or stamped with designs.

IV. Pieces are set aside to dry. — The slower and more evenly the clay dries, the less likely it is to crack. Also, pieces that are generally even in thickness are less likely to crack.

V. Dries "leather hard" ("greenware"). — A fairly air-tight cupboard is a good place to dry objects, which can be covered with a damp cloth. An empty tin can placed over the object is also good. As the object dries it can be sanded with sandpaper or sponged smooth with sponge and water.

A. Do nothing to it,
　　or

B. Texture can be incised, etc.
　　and/or

C. Engobe (colored slip "underglaze") can be painted on. — This a mat and porous cover which should be glazed in the next firing if object is to hold liquids.
　　and (if desired)

D. A pattern can be scratched through the engobe. — Technique called "sgraffito."

　　or

E. Pieces can be cut out, etc.

VI. Dries to "bone dry" (still "greenware"). — Very breakable at this point. Be careful!

A. Can be left unfired even though very breakable. — If leaving clay unfired is the original intention, mixing wheat paste with the clay at the outset would yield more permanent objects.

1. Unpainted

    or

2. Painted with tempera

    or

3. Rubbed with shoe polish or wax

    or

4. Sprayed or painted with starch or shellac

B. If moistened, can be painted with engobe.

C. Fired when "bone" dry (completely dry).

VII. First Firing (bisque or biscuit fired).

The kiln should be in a safe place. In bisque firing pieces can touch each other unless they are painted with engobe.

Pyrometric cones that melt at certain temperatures or trip-off switches help judge the amount of firing. Gradual heating up and gradual cooling off are essential.

VIII. The "bisque" ware which comes out of the first firing is then glazed.

A. Glaze

1. Applied with a soft brush (about 3 coats)

    or

2. Poured or dipped

B. Ceramic crayon (comes in different colors; gives linear effects)

C. Fired

Do not glaze undersides. Glaze can be transparent or opaque, mat or shiny, plain or multicolored—unlike "engobe" (colored slip) which always fires dull. Be sure that the glazes "fit" the clay that you are using. To insure this consult with dealers and keep samples and a log of firings.

IX. Second Firing (glaze firing or glost firing).

It is wise to paint the kiln with wash to protect it against glaze. No pieces should touch each other. Since it is difficult to know how glazes will look after they are fired it would be worthwhile to collect samples of firings.

Color

Color is a fundamental dimension in children's art work. Following is a chart which indicates the changing aspect of color use in the grades.

K	1	2	3	4	5	6
Fewer colors (starting with one color or hue)		→			The use of a greater number of colors or *HUES*	
Brighter (purer) bolder use of color		→			Use of more *TINTS* (color + white) and more *SHADES* (color + black).	
More subjective use of color		→			More objective or realistic use of color (Tied in with greater scientific knowledge of color)	
Flat and decorative use of color		→			Greater 3-d use of color, e.g., shading and color perspective (serial perspective where far-away mountains appear a dull blue). Warm colors seem to advance, cool colors recede.	

Children should be made aware of the broad aspect of color:

as nature uses color: In imitative camouflage, as a chameleon changing its color, or a deer marked with the color and pattern of its background. Color in people, the sea, flowers, the earth, grays of mountains, reds of the sunsets, reflections, etc.

as man uses color: In magazine illustrations, in science research, in paintings, in maps, in Christmas cards, in industry (for instance, complicated wiring systems), in poster design, in interior decoration, in education for social studies units (African masks, Indian headdress), etc.

Crafts

Throughout man's history he has fashioned and used objects for many purposes—magic, signs of wealth and power, toys, utility, religion, intrinsic beauty, etc. As would be expected, the artistic quality of these objects ranges from the unattractive to the beautiful and significant. Crafts can be found anywhere from the museum to the marketplace. In the making of crafts in the elementary school, the teacher should consider educational and artistic worth and the difficulty of execution in relation to the child's ability. Cost and availability of materials are also important considerations. Both craftsmanship and artistic design should always go hand in hand.

Crayons

Known as encaustic, the use of colored wax for picture-making is an ancient art. Today in the elementary schools colored wax in the form of crayons is the most popular art medium. This is understandable since crayons are inexpensive, compact, require no preparation, and are considered less "messy" than other media. However, crayons are too often used within a narrow range of techniques and used to excess, shutting out other media.

In lower grades fewer colors and larger sizes of crayons are generally used than in the upper grades. Children should be urged to combine colors rather than always to accept the colors without change as they come out of the box. It is also recommended that crayons be purchased without paper covering or that the paper be removed, so that the side of the crayons can be worked. A rectangular crayon is preferable to the round.

Cut Paper and Collage
(See Paper Sculpture)

Paste-ups, sometimes called collage, can play a large part in the elementary school art program. The emphasis ranges from the highly creative to the traditional and exacting (map work and some lettering), depending on both the grade level and the purpose. However, these activities should never result in the duplications of meaningless patterns. There are an endless number of materials that can be used—paper, wallpaper, drawings, cloth, nature forms, cardboard, etc.

Design and Composition

Design is an orderly and/or significant arrangement of such art elements as line, dark and light color texture, etc. Design can be seen in a painting, a construction of blocks on a kindergarten floor, a leaf, a shell, or whatever. An aim in education is to improve the design abilities of each child. Design can be formal (as a repeat design in cloth) or informal (as a painting by a first grader).

With children in grades K through 6 design is usually intuitive, guided by a "feeling of rightness." This is especially true of the younger child. Therefore, it is wise not to be too analytical when talking about design. Taste can be improved through evaluation and discussion.

Ask yourself and each student to think about the "rightness" of arrangement of a given problem in a given medium.

Other sections in this guide should be considered from the standpoint of the problem-solving aspect of improving design. However, remember that design cannot be learned by dependence on copying others or by depending on stereotypes.

sources for designs:

Imagination

Nature—tree shapes, leaf shapes, rock textures, butterfly patterns, fish scales, star formations, shells, snowflakes.

man-made form:

Machinery, plastics, telephone poles, trades.

art:

Paintings, tapestries, architecture, printed textiles.

The above can be presented by means of picture files, bulletin boards, music, field trips, books. Children should do "visual research" first and then try:

border designs, murals, weaving, printmaking, greeting cards, etc.

Dioramas

Dioramas, panoramas, and peep shows recreate scenes on a small scale. Because of the scales and detail these are activities more suited to grades 4 to 6. In these grades, dioramas may be representations of reality or imagination and may be done in a realistic or abstract style. They can correlate effectively with other elementary school activities:

Social Studies (agriculture in another country, rivers and dams, life in a fishing village, etc.)

Science (solar system, life cycle of a frog, etc.)

Reading (scene from a book or story, etc.)

or be part of Art (an abstract style, a copy of a mural, architecture, etc.). See chart page 67.

Drawing

Drawing is a vital language of communication to many (technical illustrators, artists, folk artists), but to most adults today it is an unused

SOME OF THE MATERIALS POSSIBLE IN THE CONSTRUCTION OF DIORAMAS AND PEEP SHOWS

CONTAINERS	BINDERS	BACKGROUNDS	MIDDLE GROUND	FOREGROUND, HOUSES, FIGURES, ANIMALS AND OTHER FORMS
paper or tagboard	glue	paper sculpture	paper sculpture	oil-base clay (as the base or for object)
shoe box	paste	rounded white paper	paper	salt and flour paste
cardboard box	staples	cardboard	cardboard	paper
hat box	tape	tracing paper	corrugated cardboard	papier mache
chip board	sewing supplies	tissue paper	nature forms	clay
	oil-base clay	plastic	mirror	cardboard
				sawdust and wheat paste
				wire
				asbestos
				nature forms
				realia
				paper sculpture
				pipe cleaners
				mirror
				plastic
				cellophane

tool. To most young children drawing is a natural form of expression; as they grow older this ability should not be lost. Each individual and each grade level present a unique problem in the teaching of drawing. The teacher must be conscious of the wide range of purposes that drawing can serve. Drawing in the scribble stage will be quite different from that of the symbolic and the dawning realism stages. The teacher must be able to help each child in his ability to draw. When a sixth grader asks, "How can I make it look right?" he needs specific help in drawing. An effective teacher should be able to draw in a wide range of styles, from the subjective to the objective.

methods of learning to draw and teaching children to draw:

Doodling. A free subconscious progression of lines and textures often results in a more significant statement than a strained attempt at "realism." This is sometimes a good way for an adult or child to get started and then to progress toward a more conscious level of drawing.

Drawing games. One child makes a scribble and another child tries to make a drawing out of it. In another game, every player draws a head at the top of the paper, which is folded at the neck line; papers are exchanged; everyone draws a body and again all is covered by folding; papers are exchanged and then the legs and feet are drawn; papers are exchanged and unfolded.

Interpretive responses to music, stories, poems, discussions, memories, the expression of moods, imagination, and dreams.

toward realism: interpretive drawing (upper grade children)

Memory drawing. The teacher holds up an object for a given length of time; the object is put away and the children try to draw it; the object is held up again, the children observe and then make corrections.

Contour drawing. Any object or person that will remain relatively still is drawn in detailed outline by concentrating on the point-by-point contour of the object and *not* looking at the paper. The proportions will probably be off but this is an excellent training for hand-eye coordination.

Gesture drawing. With pencil or pen a kinesthetic response to form and movement—a very quick, shorthand-scribble—is made of any object whether moving or not. This is very good as a starter for a drawing of a mural cartoon.

Drawing from observation. Observation is usually colored by one's interpretation. Sometimes, however, there is a need to approach objective reality (e.g., an accurate drawing in science). It is then necessary to utilize some elements of what is known as perspective. In the fifth and sixth grades most children will want to know how to use some elements of perspective. This can be learned by *observation*. Outlines of objects to be drawn can be tested by: (1) holding a pencil or ruler in front of the line to be drawn and comparing it (the degree to which it tilts in relation to the vertical and the horizontal of the paper) to the line drawn on paper; (2) comparing the angle made in an imaginary line—ruler or other straight edge—between any two (of thousands of) points in space; (3) looking through a rectangular finder (like the cardboard holder for a 35 mm. slide); it is possible to set a picture plane within a prescribed space and to establish the verticals (sides) and horizontals (top and bottom) at close proximity to the area drawn; (4) drawing on a piece of glass (that is between the observer and the area to be drawn) with a grease pencil or pointed brush and poster paint; by keeping the head at a fixed point and closing one eye it is possible to be quite accurate in outline tracing without knowing how to draw; (5) tracing lines of convergence on a photograph that includes near and far relationships, demonstrating that objects that are far away appear to be smaller; (6) giving lessons on shading and textures, rough and smooth, etc.

Finger painting is an ancient art that has become popular with fine artists and in schools (especially in the nursery and kindergarten levels) within the last few decades. Effects are quick. The directness of expression appeals to young children and is sometimes an asset in therapy techniques. Finger painting can be done by one child at a time, a group, or the entire class. The finished results can range from the nonobjective to the realistic.

paints: (consistency should be thick and cohesive)
Liquid starch and powdered tempera
Wheat paste and powdered or liquid tempera
Commercial finger paint (powder or mixed form)
Homemade starch and paint
School paste and paint or food coloring
Cornstarch and paint or food coloring
Buttermilk and paint or food coloring

surface: Special finger paint paper (glossy side up), shelf paper, white wrapping paper, crayon on any stiff paper, wall paper, butcher paper; if prints are to be made—glass, formica, masonite, linoleum.

other materials: Aprons, newspapers, rags, water, sponges.

a place to dry the work: Have it available before the work is started (newspapers on the floor, tables, or shelves; strings or wires with clothes pins, etc.)

Holidays

A holiday can be a very human expression of the religion, history, and customs of people. Through holidays children can learn much about other peoples and about their own cultural heritage. However, if tribute is paid to holidays by duplicating meaningless stereotypes, the activity has little significance to the children. This can be avoided if the teacher:
1. Remembers that themes can be traditional but art should interpret them in a fresh and original way.
2. Studies the history and meanings behind each holiday.
3. Presents material in a way that would interest children.

4. Uses good educational techniques (discussion, reports, art projects, etc.)
5. Encourages individual interpretation and exciting design instead of outworn stereotypes.
6. Does not spend more time than the material warrants.

Lettering and Poster

If grade level and individual differences are considered, teaching lettering to children need not be difficult. Use an alphabet that the children know—simple manuscript in the first grade, for example—and art techniques and standards that the children can handle. Refer to ancient (Chinese, Arabic) and contemporary calligraphers and to good commercial art. Lettering has many uses both for the teacher and the children in school.

Map Making

TWO-DIMENSIONAL		THREE-DIMENSIONAL	
tempera paint	brown paper	sand and paste	cardboard
chalk (fixed)	shelf paper	papier mache	celotex
felt pens	colored paper	(pulp or crushed	masonite
crayon	cardboard	or laminated)	plywood
water color	celotex	flour and salt	
colored pencil	window shade	celotex and paste	
cut paper	old sheet	sawdust and paste	
colored inks	tracing paper	sawdust and	
collage	oilcloth (back)	plaster	
		asbestos and paste	
		balloon and papier	
		mache (globe)	

protective materials: Saran Wrap, fixative, commercial spray (clear shellac, lacquer, varnish) is applied over the completed work or liquid starch, glue, or thin paste mixed with the paint.

methods of transfer:
Tracing (architect's tracing paper) onion skin paper
Opaque projector
Slide projector
Squares (grid)
Measure with compass, then sketch
Freehand sketch (with or without finder)
Photograph of real place or of map
Pantograph

things to check in order to achieve an attractive and functional map:

Legibility
Logical and artful arrangement
Neatness
Color selection and application
Educational aids, as required (scale, etc.)

Masks

Masks have been used for centuries by various people from the primitive (witch doctors, war dances) to the modern (parties, Mardi-Gras, and in the arts). In the schools masks can be used to enable a shy child to enter into an activity, to add to a party or holiday (Halloween), or in social studies enrichment (Mexico, Africa, Far East).

Mat and Frame

Art work, written work, photographs, or any flat work to be displayed look better when matted or framed. A properly displayed item has a mat or frame that is related to the dominant color and/or theme of the item to be mounted, and related to the general color theme in the classroom; the border is even or is wider on the bottom, or it has a special proportion that is suitable.

BASIC MATERIALS FOR A MAT OR FRAME	SHAPED	COLORED OR TEXTURED	ADHERED TO WALL, ETC. BY MEANS OF:
paper	use as is	plain	pins
cardboard	(item placed	stipple or spatter	thumb tacks
corrugated cardboard	on top)	painted	masking tape
cloth	cut (center out	glue and sand	mastic
yarn or string	in strips)	hole punch	
stiff wire	torn	sponge printed	
tape	folded	sewed	
pressed cork	scored	finger painted	
masonite	rolled out	marbleized	
plywood	sawed	yarn	
molding	moulded	shoe polish	
rope		chalk and starch	
tree branches		covered with cloth	
old movie film			
magazine photos			
papier mache			
raffia			

Mobiles

Mobiles, moving sculpture in space, are truly a product of the twentieth century. Since Alexander Calder first created them in the 1930's, mobiles have been widely seen in museums, homes, and the commercial world. Elementary school children of every age enjoy watching mobiles, but they are most successfully made by upper-grade children.

Calder's mobiles and others seen in museums are made of materials that are too difficult for children to work. If the spirit of graceful motion and the lack of heavy clutter is maintained, there are many readily available materials, such as discarded wire coathangers, twigs from trees, cardboard, driftwood, colored plastic, or empty spools.

Modeling Materials (other than clay)

The art program should not be confined to "flat work"; most children enjoy working in three-dimensional materials. The best and most often used modeling material is clay. (See sections on *Clay* and *Carving*.) In working with modeling material, children do not have to draw photographically; by the nature of the material, they start with the general and work toward the specific. In art this is a good working sequence.

some inexpensive modeling materials: (add oil of cloves and food coloring)

Flour plus an equal part of salt; mix, add water, and knead
Oil-base clays (Plastecine, Clayola, etc.)
Play-Do (expensive)
Wet sand
Shredded asbestos (wheat paste can be added)
Wheat paste plus sand or sawdust or sifted dirt or crushed leaves, etc.
Liquid starch plus sawdust, torn paper (see *Papier Mache*)

Models

If a model is made with perception and done artfully it can be a way of better understanding science or social studies. It can be a means of visualizing something larger or more complicated. Kindergarten block play often has simple elements of relatedness to the larger world. With upper-grade children model making might take the form of dioramas, panoramas, or cardboard models of houses or space rockets.

Murals

Any decoration or picture, mosaic, painting (even a stained glass window) which is on or part of a wall may be called a mural. Designing a mural is a good activity for any grade level, if the teacher keeps worthy educational goals and the ability of her students in mind.

subject matter or themes for murals: Social science units, holiday or special days, field trips, science, illustrations of stories or books, a design of the mood and rhythm of music, the life of a composer, sports, health, safety.

sequence in developing a mural: Planning stage (individual child or committee or class). Discussion of theme, materials and the wall space to be covered.

preliminary work: (Don't have this too long or detailed in order to maintain interest and spontaneity.) Sketches (individual or group); projection of sketch with opaque projector; light chalk sketch.

actual work: Individual *or* group *or* class.

Paper Sculpture

Paper sculpture is the result of techniques that transform paper from two- to three-dimensional forms. Projects can range from the realistic to the abstract. The latter style is more likely to be found in the lower grades. Paper sculpture can also become part of other art activities such as the finishing touches on papier mache animals or "3-d" lettering on bulletin boards.

Papier Mache

Papier mache is an inexpensive, versatile medium consisting of a binder (usually wheat paste) plus paper (usually newspapers). There are a variety of ways of using papier mache. The method or combination of methods that you choose should suit the grade level of your children and the project that you want to accomplish. In general, the K through 2 grades should avoid projects that would not warrant the time necessary for completion. See chart page 75.

Pencil

In general soft lead pencils (#1, 2, 2B, 3B, 4B, etc.) are better for drawing than the harder pencils (#3, 3½, H, 2H, etc.). Generally crayons are better than colored pencils, but in the upper grades colored pencils offer some children a new medium and an opportunity to achieve greater detail. Colored pencils are used mainly in the seventh and eighth grades, but do not have to be restricted to these grades.

METHODS OF USING PAPIER MACHE

METHOD	DESCRIPTION
Mash or pulp method	Paper is torn into bits (an inch or less in diameter). The paper is then soaked in water (from 1 to 24 hours); or cooked in water a couple of hours, cooled, and water squeezed out; or left alone. The paper is then combined with a mixture of wheat paste and water. This is then moulded into shape. Allow to dry; paint; varnish.
A shell put around a basic shape	Crushed tied newspapers, boxes, a stuffed paper bag, a balloon, rolls of tied newspapers, etc. form the basic shape. Strips or squares of newspapers dipped in wheat paste (consistency of thick cream) are added on top of the basic form. If the understructure is sturdy, only a couple of layers are needed; if weak, add at least five layers (the last layer of paper towels).
Objects duplicated	The above method can be used to duplicate such objects as fruit or pottery. The object is painted with a grease, then strips of paper and wheat paste are put on top of the object to the thickness of five or more. When dry, the layers are cut with a razor or sharp knife (by the teacher) into halves, the object taken out, and the halves put back together with wheat paste and strips of paper. Paint when dry.
Laminated method	This method is suitable for objects that are thin. A decorative large butterfly or the crust of mountain range on a relief map could be made in this method. Cut or tear the desired shape out of layers of newspapers, to the thickness of at least five. These layers can be wet or dry. Wheat paste (thickness of thick cream) is then painted between each layer. The form is shaped by temporarily propping up with crushed paper, tying string, etc. When dry, the laminated form will keep its shape. Paint.

If the children draw too small or too restrictively with pencil, it would be preferable for them to use media like chalk tempera or crayon. It is better not to use pencil on a preliminary drawing for water color, tempera, or crayon; it is preferable to use water color to start a water color, crayon to start crayon, etc. Here again, this is not a hard and fast rule since intention and temperament have always been basic guides for artists and children in making their own rules. It is certainly legitimate to use pencil in combination with water color, tempera, chalk, crayon, etc., as mixed media.

Puppets and Marionettes

Puppets and marionettes are an excellent way of correlating art with other subjects in the elementary school. For example, in the language

arts puppets help many shy children communicate with ease; in social studies pioneer life can be dramatically enacted through puppets; and in health education puppets made out of vegetables can show concepts of good diet. Puppets have played an important part in man's cultural history, beginning as far back as the Stone Age, when stone and amber figures were used. In the making of puppets and marionettes in the classroom, be certain that the process is geared to the children's abilities. The following chart indicates some of the construction possibilities.

KIND	WORKED BY MEANS OF:	MADE OF: (one or combination)	ATTACHED BY:
Finger puppet	Fingers and hand	Cardboard Paper Tape Cloth	Rubber band Tape
Push puppet	Stick Wire Yardstick	Paper Cardboard Papier mache	Tacks Glue Paste Tape
Hand or fist puppet	Fingers and Hand	Paper bag—Vegetable— Sock—Mitten—Glove— Paper—Papier mache— Asbestos—Bottles— Soda straws—Cloth— Sawdust and wheat paste— Bean bag—Styrofoam	Sewed Glue Tape Wheat paste
Shadow puppet	Stick Wire String	Cardboard Paper Colored cellophane	Clasps Tacks Glue Sewed

Stencil

Stenciling is a means of duplicating a design in value, color, or texture. In this capacity it is a printmaking technique; for example, silk screen is a stencil technique. Stenciling is also a means of achieving greater control or precision in selectively applying color to a surface. Stencils can be used in any grade level; however they are most commonly used in the upper grades. Either liquid paint or dry coloring media—crayon—can be used. Both that which is cut away and that which remains can be used as stencils.

Tempera Paint

Tempera is a commonly used medium that comes in powdered form (most used in elementary school because it is least expensive and is easily stored); in cake form; and in liquid form (sometimes called show card or poster paint). In the schools it is a water-base medium, although the powder can be mixed with liquid starch, shellac, varnish, or linseed oil as well.

The powder can be mixed by stirring, shaking (jar, empty milk carton), or letting it stand for a while. To hasten mixing (especially the red colors) a drop of alcohol will break down the surface tension. Oil of wintergreen or a few drops of liquid starch will prevent spoilage, but it is a good rule not to let mixed paint stand too long. The amount of water per pigment partly depends on the quality of paint (fineness of grind, brilliance of color, etc.) and the desired effect.

	WATER		DRY TEMPERA
Thick	1	to	4
Medium	2	to	3
Thin	4	to	1

Tempera paint can be applied with a brush (pointed, easel) in various ways: spatter, stipple, stroke (dry brush, loaded brush), thick or thin, or as an overglaze; it can be applied with a roller (brayer), with a rolling pin, bottle, with sponge or rag; or with a spray device (insecticide, spray gun, tooth brush, fixative blower).

Mixed with a liquid starch or casein glue with little or no water, tempera can be a covering for craft projects that will not need a protective covering.

Water Color

Water color is basically a transparent medium, in contrast to tempera. Since the colors are transparent or translucent every "mistake" is easier to detect and harder to correct than with an opaque medium. Water color comes in cake form in pans (with refills available) and also in tube form, which is rarely used in elementary schools. Some school systems do not provide water colors in the primary grades, but this need not be the case if the budget is not too tight, since, if used correctly, even kindergarten children can profit from its use. At an early age children use water colors with spontaneity and disinterest in technical perfection.

As children get older, and there is a need for more control and varied technique, the teacher can provide for this by presenting new techniques.

Weaving

Weaving is an ancient art of interlacing longitudinal materials at right angles to each other, either by hand or by the use of a loom, which can be very simple (sticks, card) or intricate (harness). The length of the woven material is limited to the length of the loom unless there are winding devices (roller or warp-beam). Weaving can be a very simple or a complicated process and can be taught in any of the grades and to the retarded, average, or gifted.

In weaving, the warp is fixed to the loom (lengthwise) and the weft or woof is interlaced back and forth across the width, pulled by hand or a shuttle. A device for separating the warp in a desired pattern across the weft is a heddle; it can be made of cardboard, strings, tongue depressors, or purchased and worked by twisting, pulling, or pressing on a foot treadle.

PLANS AND SYSTEMS

The school and the community play a strong part in the structure of the classroom, but the ultimate influence is the teacher. She is the key to the success of the art program, and unfortunately, there is no simple formula to identify the good art teacher. There are teachers who concoct personalized structures of classroom operation and there are those who work under traditional, static structures. There are those teachers who are permissive and those who are formal. Whatever the personal inclination or whatever the structure that is traditional at the school, the classroom or the special art teacher must cope with some workable system for handling art materials. In comparing teachers of different subject matter, the art teacher is probably the most individualistic. This is understandable because of the very nature of the subject, yet art materials and the aims of the art program do offer some structure of operation. As the trend toward new teaching structure permeates from the sciences toward other subjects, art will probably be the last to be affected. This is not merely because the nature of art defies categorizing. Rather it grows out of the likelihood that art teachers will fight any sort of standardization. In any event, most everyone who teaches art uses a system of one kind or another.

In the self-contained classroom a movement from one subject activity to another must be well directed. Parallel activities are even more difficult to control efficiently. Private schools, museums, neighborhood houses, recreation centers, and summer camps teach art under a variety of systems from the very informal to the formal. The public schools tend to be more formal in the management of art classes.

Variations of the individualized system of the Dalton Plan (Dalton School, New York City), where each student contracts for his own series of projects, are found in some elementary and secondary art programs. A permissive system is used in Summerhill (in England). There are many plans and many district and national policies that guide the teaching of art; no one system can be recommended exclusively.

CHAPTER FOUR   *New Horizons*

THE STRUCTURE OF ART AND NEW HORIZONS

No matter what the technological devices and no matter how enlightened the times, it is never possible to see beyond the horizon with any certainty. Nevertheless some trends that we see in art education today might give at least hints of the future. Some of these trends have been previously mentioned, but now an elaboration is in order. Art has been a part of the elementary school curriculum for decades; but, even though there has not been much change in its curriculum in the last twenty years, there has been a searching and restless quest. The hope is that out of this quest will evolve needed innovations and practices.

Art, the first language of our distant ancestors, has been with us throughout our history. The elementary, as well as the secondary and college curricula might well include a humanities time-place-line orientation from the inception of a child's school career. It would be possible and desirable for the humanities base to start this early and continue to be a reference structure for every subject at every level. We are beginning to see the weakness of stressing only the here-and-now process. Knowledge of the past and a better founded sense of the future would make the school experience of the present have more meaning. The here-and-now could be compared to the near-and-far and the long ago. A graphic time-place-line, history-culture chart or schema might find itself in the school library (which should be more than just a storehouse of books) or in a special humanities-anthropology-art room. This where-

and-when orientation chart would help to relate facts and skills of writing, reading, science, social sciences, art, and music. Reproductions (records and tapes of music and prints of art) would be milestones in our cultural history. We conform to the bullying influence of the school clock as it ticks off the compartments of subject periods; yet we need a time clock that would allow for a maplike orientation of the total context of our heritage. In the structure of our knowledge there are two elements that are primary: the contextual relativity of any "subject," e.g., art as it relates to all else; and the element of time and place. For this reason the structure of the teaching of any subject matter in the elementary school should provide an ever-present map that encompasses the context, time, and place of every fact and concept. A culture map of some kind might someday be in every school. As museums, libraries, fairs, and other institutions increasingly realize their educational responsibility, the gap between them and the schools lessens. The future should bring fruitful partnerships between schools and other institutions.

Art would play a primary part in the context-time base of the humanities core. Within the realm of the laboratory practice of art lies another structural base. In a coordinated core of fine and applied arts the art laboratory finds roots and stimulus in the humanities map but the direction is always guided by the individual determinism of the students. Articulation in art education, starting in preschool programs ideally, should be an unencumbered aesthetic journey reaching formal culmination in college. By the time a student enters college he would speak the natural language of fine and applied art through painting, drawing, printmaking, crafts (weaving, ceramics, etc.), design, lettering and other applied arts. Both the college-bound and terminal student would have been required to have had—along with foreign language and mathematics —elementary school art throughout the grades and two years of art in high school. More concentrated courses would be available for the student who intends to be an art major.

The groundwork for an articulated structure of art education needs to be established now. Just as mathematicians have helped to fashion "new math" curricula for elementary schools, it is not too early for fine artists, commercial artists, college art teachers, classroom teachers, and art educators to structure basic requirements for all students and for the art majors. The unique way artists work, the products of their work, the way anthropologists find art in various cultures, and the nature of applied arts of our own time, all would contribute to revitalizing art curriculum and education in the future. Those working in research in art education and allied areas will continue to point the way. Legislation and grants will continue to support these efforts. Such agencies are realizing that sciences must be balanced by the arts. The overspecialization now being received by many students in the sciences must have the mediating properties of the humanities and the performing arts.

THE STUDENT AND NEW HORIZONS

Universal literacy is closer than ever to being achieved in this country; the new major thrust in education is increasing the depth of subject matter and starting the education process at an earlier age. Art has always had a home in what is now the preschool program. As predicted by some, the formal school might start as early as two years of age, and at this level art could easily be included in the curriculum through projects in drawing, painting, and constructing.

Psychological studies and the construction of tests are broadening our knowledge of the child. Lately I.Q. has been universally considered as an attempt to measure only one of many potentials and characteristics of the child. The recognition and measurement of the creativity syndrome today is assuming increasing importance in education and industry. Research of Guilford and Torrance has shown that problem-solving and creativity have a common source and that experience in one assists the other.

The student of the future will be expected to acquire an increasing body of knowledge and at the same time—with the help of more realistic and sophisticated teaching methods, better systems of knowledge, and the use of new teaching devices—he should learn and perform better in art as well as in other subjects. With what seems to be an increasing cultural maturity in this country, art should not only be more readily palatable but also more persistently reinforced through the avenues of mass media and, ideally, through the influence in the home. It is true that in the transition to greater racial equality, there might be a temporary lag of social impetus, but in the long run there should be a stimulating cross-culturalization that should result in social and intellectual advances. Living in a democratic society that is undergoing drastic social and technological changes necessitates the training of artists who can graphically depict change and an aesthetically educated population who can be enlightened witnesses to change. Art, as a universal language should have more use and meaning. The humanities and the use of the articulated laboratory curriculum mentioned in the previous section would be ready vehicles to help prepare the citizen of tomorrow for his increasing leisure time and more sober responsibility.

THE TEACHER AND NEW HORIZONS

In increasing amounts the general classroom teacher and the special art teacher will be pressed to structure and articulate the art program in the elementary grades. Otherwise, teachers will run the risk of not having time to teach art and leaving it out of the curriculum entirely. The administration and the teachers in the self-contained classroom will have to plan the art program very carefully.

It would seem that team teaching and teaching by subject matter specialists will increase in grades 4 and above. This system will probably insure allegiance to art in a real, rather than watered-down, sense, and it should also guarantee more qualified art teaching. This implies that the training of art teachers for the elementary grades will be more systematic and intensive. Teacher training is presently taking a longer time and more demands are being made on students. In addition to offering a thorough liberal arts training, teacher education now tends to require fewer education courses, as much or more student teaching, and more emphasis on academic majors and minors. Art is being considered an academic subject in many states, and thus is being given a more serious status.

It might even be that in the future an artist-in-residence might be possible for brief periods in the upper grades of the elementary school. This possibility is not too far-fetched, since the work of contemporary artists and the way that these artists work is often more understandable to children than to the majority of adults.

Methods of teaching art will come under revision in the future. The laboratory method should persist but it should become a more pressured search for perfection on individual terms. The strategy of the method will probably be influenced by the advanced methods being used for science and social studies. The climate for the acceptance of art should continue to improve and this will make the teaching of art less a matter of apology and more a matter of serious purpose. With the increase of museum attendance and general interest in art, the tide will turn away from the present lassitude in art teaching. Direction by teachers of art will be needed, and the teaching of art will become more confident and demonstrative. The schools must catch up with our age and use dimensions that include more than lecture and the printed word.

THE CLASSROOM AND NEW HORIZONS

The use of new forms of teaching environment might be one of the most novel changes in the future. The art in architecture—more artful design and embellishments such as mosaics—should become more prevalent. The regular, rectangular classroom should give way to new and more imaginative forms. School plants are already being more flexibly designed—sometimes around a circular core. Form, function, and aesthetic consideration for the special needs of the elementary school are being taken into consideration.

It is hoped that in the future there will be a special art room in every school with a special art teacher in charge. Here art equipment, sufficient storage space, and flexibility for individual and group work areas would be planned for. Provisions for outdoor sculpture and craft work could extend from the central indoor work area.

In the future, schools should look less like factories and more like exciting work areas. Building and landscaping in progress might be a feature of such a school; a joint project of teacher and students might be the building of a giant relief map of the country or the continent; or, an imitation of a Mexican marketplace might be built where the children would only speak Spanish.

Because of the increasing population, one of the functional problems for architects and educators to solve is a more practical utilization of space. Rooftop playgrounds and pedestrian overpasses might enter into the solution. The use of new construction materials might allow for varied design and the greater functional use of space. The need in many urban and some rural areas for additional adult education and for a focus for neighborhood coordination might be met by the local elementary school building being used at night and on weekends. Here adult classes would be given in needed subjects and on appropriate levels, school orientation and parent-teacher opportunities for cooperative projects would be offered. With these neighborhood programs underway, joint programs between schools would be more feasible and desirable. Art would serve with exhibits and decorations and with the production of instructional materials. Parents in the adult education classes could produce many functional materials while learning skills and a trade. The greatest need (and the place to start) will be in the economically depressed areas.

There are many ideas on the drawing boards but local financial support is often lacking. A greater volume of money is needed even to keep up with population increases and the replacement of outworn facilities. It seems likely that government support will increase, making it possible to meet these needs and to make some of the new ideas a reality.

THE DYNAMIC STRUCTURE OF ART EDUCATION AND NEW HORIZONS

Method in the teaching of art in the elementary school will always be an individual matter—probably more individual than in any other subject area. The teacher will be guided by personal philosophy and

particular art strengths. Thus, standardization of scope and sequence is difficult in the elementary school art program. Art teachers have always fought standardization and usually with good cause; however, in the future, unity of purpose and an art program that will coordinate with the total program will be essential if art is to assume its proper place in the elementary school. If this is done with the help of art teachers, the spirit and content of the program should not be sacrificed.

In the future the laboratory should have more sustained purpose. The restless performance of one project after another should give way to a more systematic development of a language of communication through art. Children would find meaning in basic modes of expression ranging from the subjective to the objective in drawing, painting, print-making, crafts, and lettering. These would be developed with particular attention to individual differences among children.

Fine arts, applied arts and industrial arts might work closer together in a coordinated team, and such a fusion might be influential in modifying the elementary school curriculum in the next twenty years. This along with other influences would make the methods of elementary school art less static.

The future should continue to see controversy between exponents of the laboratory method and of the static, rote-lecture method of teaching. It would seem that the laboratory method will persist and become more dominant in art as well as all other subject areas. Because of the nature of the subject, the art laboratory will always be the favored method.

An added ingredient in the elementary school curriculum may very well be the humanities orientation. At present some secondary schools are moving in this direction, even if slowly. If a greater emphasis on the humanities or the anthropology point of view is to be felt in the elementary school, a lecture-discussion-laboratory method might well be developed.

The method of learning by doing has never become completely outmoded. In recent years art education has been influenced by the research in art education, done primarily by people in psychology. The emphasis is usually on individual differences and the general nature of learning. The implication often is that the teacher should prepare a custom-made educational package hoping to hit the individual mark. To structure subject matter into a more consumable form, as suggested by Bruner's and McLuhan's writings, could be a good influence if the aims of art education are not violated. A new wave of writings by art educators, rather than psychologists, has been a provocative influence. Each one of these influences should eventually result in an effective and more unified art program.

A work of art is a reservoir of many meanings to many people and the engineering of a work of art demands total involvement. In other subjects, to a greater extent than in art, the usual linear quality of the printed word and the linear quality of the teacher's lecture is the common method of education. This process of education is much like a deep sea diver who is very limited in his breathing, walking, and feed-back communication. In a truly supportive atmosphere the problem-solving environment should completely involve the students. More efficient learning and participation with less likelihood of dropping out of the track should result. For example, rather than a lecture or a single reading on ancient Egypt there would be a dynamic audio-visual presentation, with opportunity for student interaction, so that the life and arts of Egypt would have an educational impact not otherwise possible. Technologically this country has the wealth and equipment to do much more than this in education. The transportation and the communication industries, for example, have kept pace with technological development while education is far behind, in spite of its scale and importance. The involvement principle would take advantage of technology in fashioning giant teaching machines that would be functional school houses. Just as television has been used for good as well as harm, this direction in education could yield more efficient and exciting education or it could result in a harmful, overbearing "1984" conditioning. The not too distant future, we would hope, will bring an evolution away from the linear and static classroom to more dynamic and technologically sophisticated environments for art education and the total curriculum.

Bibliography

A. GENERAL

Barkan, Manuel, THROUGH ART TO CREATIVITY. Boston: Allyn & Bacon, Inc., 1960. By taking a camera and a tape recorder into several classrooms, the author has compiled material to show good teaching in detail.

Conant, Howard, and Arne Randall, ART IN EDUCATION. Peoria, Ill.: Chas. A. Bennett, 1959, 1963. Art from preschool through graduate study, with attention to art in the community.

Conrad, George, THE PROCESS OF ART EDUCATION IN THE ELEMENTARY SCHOOL. Englewood Cliffs, N.J.: Prentice-Hall, Inc., 1964. Psychological process of art education written for the teacher and the curriculum supervisor.

D'Amico, Victor, CREATIVE TEACHING IN ART. Scranton, Penn.: International Textbook Co., 1953. Relates the practices of professional art to the teaching of art.

De Francesco, Italo L., ART EDUCATION—ITS MEANS AND ENDS. New York: Harper & Row, Publishers, 1958. Philosophy and process of art education from the elementary grades through college.

De Long, Patrick D., Robert E. Enger, and Robert Thomas, ART AND MUSIC IN THE HUMANITIES. Englewood Cliffs, N.J.: Prentice-Hall, Inc., 1966. A general introduction to the study of humanities.

Eisner, E. W., and B. W. Ecker, READINGS IN ART EDUCATION. Waltham, Mass., Blaisdell Publishing Co., 1966. An excellent overview to the field of art education. The readings include areas in philosophy and psychology of art, criticism, and aesthetics.

Erdt, Margaret H., TEACHING ART IN THE ELEMENTARY SCHOOL. New York: Holt, Rinehart & Winston, Inc., 1957. Elementary art closely related to social studies.

Gaitskell, Charles D., CHILDREN AND THEIR ART. New York: Harcourt, Brace & World, Inc., 1958. Democratic idealism and the theory and practice of art education.

Jefferson, Blanche, TEACHING ART TO CHILDREN. Boston: Allyn & Bacon, Inc., 1963. A good stress on creativity in teaching.

Kaufman, Irving, ART AND EDUCATION IN CONTEMPORARY CULTURE. New York: The Macmillan Company, 1966. A serious and competent work on the philosophical and sociological aspects of art education.

Lark-Horovitz, Betty, Hilda P. Lewis, and Mark Luca, UNDERSTANDING CHILDREN'S ART FOR BETTER TEACHING. Columbus, Ohio: Charles E. Merrill Books, Inc., 1967. Art education research and practice in the elementary grades.

Lewis, Hilda P., editor, Preface by Mark Luca, CHILD ART—THE BEGINNINGS OF SELF AFFIRMATION. Berkeley, Calif.: Diablo Press, 1966. A University of California Extension Symposium, which featured lectures by Herbert Read, Victor D'Amico, Arno Stern, Rhoda Kellogg, and others.

Lowenfeld, Victor, YOUR CHILD AND HIS ART. New York: The Macmillan Company, 1957. Stresses the psychological basis of child art from the first scribbles of children through high school.

McFee, June King, PREPARATION FOR ART. San Francisco: Wadsworth Publishing Co., 1961. Anthropological and psychological bases of the creative process in art.

Mendelowitz, Daniel M., CHILDREN ARE ARTISTS. Stanford, Calif.: Stanford University Press, 1963. Art education from early age through senior high school.

Michael, John A., ART EDUCATION IN THE JUNIOR HIGH SCHOOL. Washington, D.C.: The National Art Education Association, 1964. A good introduction to the problems and issues involved in teaching junior high school art.

National Art Education Association, CURRICULUM DEVELOPMENT IN ART EDUCATION. Washington, D.C.: The Association, 1962. A 32-page paperback annotated bibliography of recent curriculum materials and special projects.

Read, Herbert, EDUCATION THROUGH ART. New York: Pantheon Books, Inc., 1956. A philosophic and idealistic treatment of art, the schools, and society.

Wachowiak, Frank, and Theodore Ramsay, EMPHASIS: ART. Scranton, Penn.: International Textbook Co., 1965. A very lucid description of a quality art program. The illustrations are excellent.

B. SCHOOL GUIDES AND
SCHOOL SERIES

Castro Valley School District, Mark Luca, editor, ART GUIDE—GRADES K-6. Castro Valley, Calif.: Castro Valley School District, 1960. In binder form; grade levels are related to an alphabetical coverage of art education areas.

Fearing, Kelly, Clyde Martin, Evelyn Beard, and Hans Beacham, OUR EXPANDING VISION (series). Austin, Texas: W. S. Benson and Co., 1960. Grades 1 to 6; booklets for children with a mixture of related examples of work by artists and by children.

Jefferson, Blanche, MY WORLD OF ART (series). Boston: Allyn & Bacon, Inc., 1963. Accompanying teacher's manual and a booklet for students in grades 1 to 6.

Los Angeles City Schools, ART K-2 (1962), ART 3-6 (1964), and ART FOR JUNIOR HIGH SCHOOL. Los Angeles: Los Angeles City Schools. All good guides that are nicely printed.

New York City, ART IN THE ELEMENTARY SCHOOLS. New York: Board of Education, 1964. An excellent guide for teaching art in the elementary school.

Oakland School District, Elementary Curriculum Guide, CRAFTS FOR GRADES K-6. Oakland, Calif.: Oakland Schools, 1965. Sequential photographs of elementary school crafts' processes.

Oregon State Department of Education, ART EDUCATION IN OREGON ELEMENTARY SCHOOLS. Salem, Oregon: State Board of Education, 1958 and later editions. A short but well-designed booklet, with good philosophy and excellent examples of children's work.

San Francisco Unified School District, A GUIDE FOR THE TEACHING OF ART. San Francisco: S.F. Unified School District, 1956 and several later editions. Grades K to 6; good sections on age levels and sections on posters, clay, printmaking [original examples by children], etc.; 359 pages with colored paper sections.

C. SPECIAL AREAS

DeLong, Patrick O., and Robert Thomas, ART AND MUSIC IN THE HUMANITIES. Englewood Cliffs, N.J.: Prentice-Hall, Inc., 1966. Art is first half of book and music is second half. Good treatments of both disciplines with likenesses and differences.

Hill, Edward, THE LANGUAGE OF DRAWING. Englewood Cliffs, N.J.: Prentice-Hall, Inc., 1966. Advanced for direct use for elementary schools, but an excellent teacher's guide in drawing.

Holme, Bryan, PICTURES TO LIVE WITH. New York: The Viking Press, Inc., 1959. Several examples of fine folk art. The selection has appeal and the text is good in quality.

La Mancusa, Katherine C., SOURCE BOOK FOR ART TEACHERS. Scranton, Penn.: International Textbook Co., 1965. An exposition of terms used by artists and teachers in relationship to materials used in the performance of the creative act.

Lanier, Vincent, FINAL REPORT OF THE USES OF NEWER MEDIA IN ART EDUCATION PROJECT. Washington, D.C.: National Art Education Association, 1966. A symposium directed toward the examination of the impact of educational technology on the teaching of art.

Mattil, Edward L., MEANING IN CRAFTS (2nd ed.). Englewood Cliffs, N.J.: Prentice-Hall, Inc., 1965. Good aims and examples of crafts in sculpture, printmaking, puppetry, ceramics, papier mache, etc.

National Art Education Association, STUDIES IN ART EDUCATION. Washington, D.C.: N.A.E.A. issues from 1960–1967. Art education research.

Piaget, Jean, THE CHILD'S CONCEPTION OF SPACE. London: Routledge & Kegan Paul, Ltd., 1956. A descriptive investigation of children's conception of space by a renowned developmental psychologist.

Roth, Alfred, THE NEW SCHOOLHOUSE (rev. ed.). New York: Frederick A. Praeger, Inc., 1966. Text in English, French, and German, illustrating new concepts in school architecture throughout the world.

Stevens, Harold, WAYS WITH ART . . . 50 TECHNIQUES FOR TEACHING CHILDREN. New York: Reinhold Pub. Corp., 1963. Many photographs and good text of two- and three-dimensional processes and work by children.

U.S. Committee for UNICEF, HI NEIGHBOR (series). New York, United Nations: U.S. Committee for UNICEF. Each book treats the arts and life of five United Nations countries. Some books have accompanying phonograph records of songs from the countries.

Glossary

Aerial Perspective Sometimes called "color perspective." Where to the camera, colors in the distance appear lighter and dull blue and where yellows and reds have faded. See "linear perspective."

Aesthetics The philosophic study of rightness or beauty in art.

Analogous Colors Colors closely related to each other on the color wheel, for example, red, purple, and blue.

Appreciation In the aesthetic context, to recognize the worth of something, to value it highly, to appraise or estimate its worth.

Armature A structure (of wire, wood, etc.) for the support of sculptural materials, such as clay.

Articulation The scope and sequence in the curriculum where relationships are seen from one grade level to another.

Balance In a two- or three-dimensional work of art, the relationships of the parts, which can lean toward "symmetrical" balance (one part a duplicate or mirror image of the other) or "asymmetrical" balance.

Batik On fabric (but sometimes on paper) wax or paraffin is used to resist paint, dye, or ink to produce designs on the unwaxed areas.

Biscuit or Bisque The first firing of clay in a kiln or the resultant state of the clay after the first firing.

Brayer A roller of rubber or gelatin used to apply ink to printing surfaces and, sometimes, used in place of a brush for painting.

Casting Plaster of Paris or casting plaster mixed with water is poured into a mold. When "set" or hardened it is taken out of the mold as a solid.

Ceramics The ancient art of shaping, finishing, and firing clay.

Chalk Pigment in a dry, pressed square or round form used for drawing, which, in combination with liquids, can have a painting quality.

Cognition The processes that include perception, conceptualizing, knowing, as well as judging and reasoning.

Collage   From the French word for "paste up," consists of combining pieces of cloth, magazines, drawings, and paintings.

Complementary Colors   Colors that are opposite each other on the color wheel, for example, red and green.

Composition   A significant arrangement of lines, areas, colors, and/or forms.

Contour Drawing   An outline drawing which shows the interrelationship of forms.

Dawning Realism or Preadolescent Stage   A way of drawing characteristic in the 9 to 12 age group or within the grades 3 to 7 range, which shows an attempt at realistic drawing in contrast to the schematic or symbolic methods of the previous stage.

Developmental Art Stages   Most children, whatever their background, move from the scribble to the schematic or symbolic stage and then to the dawning realism or preadolescent or true-to-appearance stage.

Diorama   A small scale realistic or interpretive model mode with art materials and/or realia within a space—usually a small box.

Elementary School   Usually grades kindergarten through 6th and sometimes 8th.

Encaustic   The ancient art of using colored wax for picture-making. Wax crayons can be adapted to this use.

Engobe   Colored, liquid clay or "slip" that is used to paint designs on ceramics before the first firing.

Evaluation   The attempt to grade or rank a work or a performance. In art, where values are changing and subjective, evaluation is difficult. (See the section on "Evaluation," II, B, 3.)

Form   Two- or three-dimensional shape or area. Sometimes "form" is used as a synonym for a total composition in art.

Gesture Drawing   A very quick, shorthand drawing, which is a kinesthetic response to form and movement rather than a studied reporting.

Glaze   (1) In water color or oil painting, a translucent layer of color. (2) In ceramics, a translucent or opaque covering of a prebaked (bisque, fired) piece of clay that must be fired again to convert it from a water soluble liquid to a hard shiny or mat crust.

Greenware   Clay before it is fired.

Hue   The name of a color, e.g., red, blue, yellow. It is sometimes called "chroma."

In-service Training   Usually a class conducted by a school system or a college for teachers who are already employed.

Intensity   The color brightness.

Kiln   A baking oven for clay or metal.

Linear Perspective   In drawing, a method of creating an illusion of depth by means of converging lines. See "Aerial Perspective."

Loop Films   Usually 8 mm. film is used in a special projector with special reels that do not need threading and permit continual showings of a film about four minutes long.

Marionettes   Figures manipulated by strings, sometimes made in the upper grades with stuffed cloth, wood, or modeling materials.

Mat   A cardboard or paper frame for a displaying of a drawing or painting. Also an adjective: lack of luster, dull.

Medium   (pl.: media)   The vehicle material in two-and three-dimensional art work—clay, paint, etc.

Mobile   An interrelationship of shapes (paper, cardboard, wood, metal, etc.) suspended by thread and free moving.

Modeling Material   A material that is pushed and pulled into the desired shape. Most modeling materials harden when the water evaporates (clay, wheatpaste plus sawdust) but some do not harden and can be reshaped (Plastecine, Clayola, sculptor's clay).

Murals   From the Latin meaning "wall," consists of painting, collage; or bas-relief modeling material—done directly on the wall or on a surface that can be applied to a wall.

Panoramas   A diorama-like small model without walls so that it can be seen from all sides.

Pantograph   A device of pieces of wood with moving joints which can trace a drawing into a larger or smaller scale.

Papier Mache   (Sometimes written papier-mâché) An ancient art which consists of paper and a binder (usually wheatpaste) shaped by modeling or stripping into shape.

Perceptual   Relating to associations with any stimulus through the senses.

Plaster of Paris   A powder which when mixed with water will harden into a chalklike solid. Casting plaster is a similar material, which is more often used in schools.

Projector—motion picture   In elementary schools a 16 mm. size film is the most common rather than the commercial 35 mm. An innovation is the 8 mm. projector or a single loop device, where about four minutes of film can be run from start to finish and directly into start again.

Projector—opaque   Pages of books, drawings, paintings, and small specimens are placed inside the opaque projector, and with a powerful light, mirror, and lens the image is projected on a screen. Since reflected light rather than transmitted light (as in the slide, overhead, and motion picture projectors) appears, the image is fainter.

Projector—overhead   A strong light source at the base of the projector is directed upward through a glass opening that is horizontal and can hold large translucent slidelike surfaces. A sheet of plastic on this opening can receive lithographic pencil writing and other opaque and translucent art materials like felt pens. These markings, after going through a wide angle lens and reflected from a mirror, are projected.

Projector—slide   Usually 35 mm. (black and white or color) translucent slides are projected upon a screen or improvised surface. Slides can be changed manually or by electrical impulses.

Puppets   Acting figure, usually worked directly by hand (contrasted to marionettes, worked by strings), made out of any of a variety of materials—paper, cloth, wood, modeling materials, etc.

Realia   Real material, such as adobe and branches of trees used in dioramas and other elementary art projects.

Self-contained Classroom   A classroom where one teacher is responsible for teaching all the subjects.

Shade   A color with a mixture of black.

Shellac   A paint, usually used without pigment as a protective coating over art work. Its solvent is alcohol and in a diluted form it is sometimes called fixative and sprayed on surfaces.

Slip   A thick liquid made of clay and water that is used in processes of making ceramic pieces.

Stencil   An art process in which an area is cut or torn out of paper so that paint (or other art media) can be applied selectively and in repetition.

Tempera   Pigment (which usually comes in powdered form) mixed with water; it is the most commonly used paint in the elementary schools.

Texture   The sensations of touch in a sculpture or the illusions of touch differences in a drawing or painting.

Tint   A color with the addition of white.

Value   The lightness or darkness of a color, or in a black-and-white drawing or print the degree of whiteness or blackness.

Varnish   A paint (like shellac) used as a protective coating over paintings or drawings. It is soluable in turpentine or paint thinner.

Video Tape   As with the sound tape recorder, a magnetic tape is able to record, store, and recreate not only the sound but also the picture of television programs. As equipment is becoming less expensive and more portable, its use in colleges and elementary schools is more likely.

Water Color   A translucent, water-base paint that comes in pans containing cakes of colors. Professional artists usually use water color from tubes.

Weld   The process of working two surfaces of clay together using slip and pressure.

Index

r5-400